CONTRO-
VERSY
DIALOGUE
AND
THE NEW
ARAB MAN

CEMAM REPORTS

Summer and Autumn **2/73**

Center for the Study
of the Modern Arab World
Saint Joseph's University, Beirut

DAR EL-MASHREQ PUBLISHERS, BEIRUT, LEBANON

CONTROVERSY DIALOGUE AND THE NEW ARAB MAN

CEMAM REPORTS

2/73

Summer and Autumn

Center for the Study
of the Modern Arab World

Saint Joseph's University, Beirut

DAR EL-MASHREQ PUBLISHERS, BEIRUT, LEBANON

ISBN 2-7214-5211-8

TABLE OF CONTENTS

PRESS SOURCES: ABBREVIATIONS AND TENDENCIES

N.B.

- Unless otherwise noted, the newspapers listed below are Beirut Arabic dailies. (w = weekly; b = bi-monthly)
- Unless otherwise indicated, the dates given with press sources are the dates of publication (not of occurrence).
- In dates, the order is: day/month. E.g. 1/12 = Dcc. 1.

AH		al-Ahram.......	(Cairo) semi-official.
AKH	w	al-Akhbar	Organ of Lebanese Communist Party.
AN	w	al-Anba........	Organ of Progressive Socialist Party (K.Jumblatt).
AW		al-Anwar.......	independent, leftist.
BAL	w	al-Balagh	independent, leftist, pro-Algerian.
BD		al-Ba'th.......	(Damascus) official Ba^{c}thist.
BIN	w	al-Bina........	Organ of Syrian Socialist Party. (PPS)
BM	w	Beirut al-Masa	Leftist, pro-Libyan.
HAD	w	al-Hadaf.......	Organ of Popular Front for Liberation of Palestine.
HAY		al-Hayat.......	Conservative, pro-Western.
HAW	w	al-Hawadith	Center right.
HUR		al-Hurriya.....	Organ of Organization of Communist Action in Lebanon, extreme left.
JB		al-Jumhurriya..	(Baghdad) governmental.
MUH		al-Muharrir	Lebanese left, pro-Palestinian, pro-Syrian Ba^{c}th.
N		al-Nida........	Organ of Lebanese Communist Party.
NAH		al-Nahar.......	Liberal, pro-Western.
OJ		l'Orient-le jour	(in French) Liberal, pro-Western.
RA		al-Ra'y al-^{c}Amm..	(Kuwait)
RAY	w	al-Raya........	Organ of Salah Jadid Section of Ba^{c}th Party.
SAFA		al-Safa	(in French) liberal, pro-Western.
SAM	w	Samedi.........	(in French) Supplement of L'Orient-le Jour
SAY	w	al-Sayyad......	independent, Lebanese nationalist.
SHIH	b	al-Shihab	conservative Muslim Sunnite; presents Muslim Brother's ideology.
TB		al-Thawra......	(Baghdad) official Iraqi Ba^{c}th.
TD		al-Thawra......	(Damascus) organ of Ba'thist Party.
YOM	w	al-Yom	independent, "Progressive", pro-Iraqi Ba^{c}th.
SUP		(Supplement)	

ABBREVIATIONS

AFPPR	-Arab Front for Participation in the Palestine Revolution
AUB	-American University of Beirut
ASU	-Arab Socialist Union
BAU	-Beirut Arab University
BUC	-Beirut University College (formerly Beirut College for Women)
CP	-Communist Party
CPC	-Certificate of Professional Competence
FFWP	-Federation of Forces of Working People
FNS	-Front for National Struggle
GWF	-General Federation of Workers
IC	-International College
IFA	-Institute of Fine Arts
ILO	-International Labor Organization
ISS	-Institute of Social Sciences
KDP	-Kurdish Democratic Party
LCP	-Lebanese Communist Party
LU	-Lebanese University
LWU	-Lebanese Writers Union
NFLUS	-National Federation of Lebanese University Students
NFU	-National Federation of Workers' and Employees' Unions
NLP	-National Liberal Party
OCAL	-Organization of Communist Action in Lebanon
OPEC	-Organization of Petroleum Exporting Countries
PDFLP	-Popular Democratic Front for the Liberation of Palestine
PFLP	-Popular Front for the Liberation of Palestine
PRFLP	-Popular Revolutionary Front for the Liberation of Palestine
PSP	-Popular Socialist Party
Rev.CC	-Revolutionary Command Council
SCIA	-Supreme Council for Islamic Affairs
SIC	-Supreme Islamic Council
SNSP	-Syrian Nationalist Socialist Party
UDY	-Union of Young Democrats
UNISOB	-UN Eco.-Social Office, Beirut
UNSC	-UN Security Council
UNWRA	-UN Works and Relief Agency
WAFA	-Palestine News Agency

A-	-Abdul
Admin.	-Administration
Amb.	-Ambassador
Assn.	-Association
Asst.	-Assistant
CC.	-Central Committee
CHRON.	-CEMAM Chronology
Com.	-Committee
Conf.	-Conference
Dir.	-Director
DG	-Director-General
Ed.	-Education
Esp.	-Especially
Exec.	-Executive
FA	-Foreign Affairs
FacEd	-Faculty of Education
Gen.	-General
GenCom.	-General Command
Gvt.	-Government
HighCL	-High Cost of Living
Info.	-Information
Intl.	-International
LL.	-Lebanese Pounds
Mil.	-Military
Min.	-Ministry
Muh.	-Muhammad
Natl.	-National
NC	-National Command
Orgn.	-Organization
PM	-Prime Minister
Pres.	-President
RC	-Regional Command
R-table	-Round Table
SecGen.	-Secretary-General
U.	-University
VP	-Vice-President

INTRODUCTION

This issue of CEMAM Reports is the second of a series. The first was entitled Tensions in Middle East Society: Winter-Spring 1972-1973, an experimental (mimeographed) collection of nine articles based on the Arab press.

This second number, which covers the summer and autumn of 1973, reflects the same interests and is based on the same sources.

The articles in CEMAM Reports, as the Introduction of the first issue explained, grew out of the review of the Arab press being carried out by members and associates of CEMAM, the Center for the Study of the Modern Arab World, at St. Joseph's University, in Beirut, Lebanon.

Items of interest regarding events and statements connected with Arab society and culture, which are chosen from selected Arab dailies, weeklies, and monthlies, are recorded on file cards to provide a continuing documentation of Arab society in change for use by the members of the Center and for visiting scholars.

The chronicles, documents and the chronology presented in this volume illustrate the values of the Arab press as a source for studying the process of change. In addition, they offer information for those who cannot read the Arabic press, and basic documentation for students of Arab society.

While chronologies of political and economic events and data are available in Western languages, it is difficult to find informative chronologies or chronicles with a socio-cultural orientation. It is this gap which CEMAM would like to fill. The categories of problems that are of special interest to CEMAM are those contained in the Center's bibliography, Arab Culture and Society in Change (Beirut: Dar el-Mashreq, 1973).

The choice of the newspapers covered is governed by several factors.

-Language: with the exception of the French dailies, l'Orient-LeJour and al-Safa, the press covered is Arabic.

-Variety of view-point: for this the Beirut press is particularly useful; the relative absence of censorship and the multiplicity of daily papers (there are over 40 licenses issued) allow the expression of almost all significant points of view.

-*Availability*: while it is usually possible to receive Middle Eastern newspapers regularly, e.g. *al-Ahram* (Cairo), *al-Ba'th* (Damascus), *al-Thawra* (Baghdad), etc., the North African are more difficult to come by. Also, there is the limitation of time and manpower.

The fact that the source of the chronicles is the press suggests some obvious limitations in the chronicles and chronology. On the other hand, precisely because the newspapers reviewed reflect varying political tendencies, a certain built-in corrective is supplied.

CONTROVERSY OVER "THE ARABISM OF THE AVANT-GARDE AND THE ISLAMISM OF THE MASSES"

An article by Munaḥ Solḥ with

two replies by ^{c}Uthman ^{c}Uthman

INTRODUCTION

by JOSEPH P. O'KANE, S.J.

The previous issue of CEMAM Reports presented a round table discussion by a group of Egyptian intellectuals on the role of religion in the modern Arab scientific society.[1] The article translated here, with the two replies to it, discusses a related question, i.e. the role of Islam in the Arab movement of national liberation.

Arab thinkers of the "progressive" school have tended to be wary of linking Arab nationalism with Islam, preferring to define Arab national identity in terms of common cultural and social heritage, common language, common historical experience, common ways of thinking and feeling, and common present and future interests, including concern for the liberation of the Arab world from imperialist domination, epitomized during the last decades in the Zionist occupation of Palestine. To the oft-repeated assertion that Islamism is a central and inseparable part of Arabism, the progressive Arab nationalist replies (with ^{c}Uthmān ^{c}Uthmān in his first reply to Munaḥ Solḥ's article): "Religion is the relation between man and his God, whereas the policy of a nation is the connection between rule, the governing power, and the governed, and between the governing power and other nations and regimes," [2] and "The Arab revolution does not believe in the mixing of politics and the religious message." [3] Among the reasons for this secularizing tendency are the following: the influence of Western models of secular national states; the danger that Arab reaction might exploit Islamic sentiment for its own interests, to the detriment of the revolution; the presence in the Arab world of numerous non-Muslims, and of religious agnostics, who would not be eligible for participation in the Arab nationalist movement if Islamism were included in the definition of Arabism. It should also be recalled that some of the leading lights in the Arab nationalist movement, including Michel ʿAflāq the Syrian Christian co-founder and ideologist of the Baʿth party, have been non-Muslims.

It is with refusal of the progressives to admit Islam as an essential element in Arabism that Munaḥ Solḥ takes issue in the present article. According to him, this refusal has been a strategic weakness in the Arab liberation movement, for it is only by appealing to the grass-roots Islam of the masses that the Arab revolution will gain for itself the vitality and momentum of an authentic mass-movement. In expounding this argument, Solh makes the following significant points:

- The Islamism of the masses is not something essentially different from the Arabism advocated by the avant-garde intellectuals. The values, concepts and heritage contained in the two are identical, except that the masses - both in the Maghrib and the Mashriq - call it Islam, rather than Arabism.

- Islam is a more authentic rallying point for the Arab masses than the nationalist ideas which "the cultured Westernized and pretentious avant-garde" have imported from the West.

- If the Islamism of the masses already contains the national goals and values advocated by the avant-garde Arab nationalists, it follows that the process known as "Arabization" is unnecessary, artificial and obstructive of the revolution.

- The present juncture of Arab history is ideally suited for enlisting the vitality of popular Islam in the cause of the Arab revolution. The days when Islamism was associated with Arab reaction have passed. Indeed, both progressive and reactionary Arab regimes have gone so far in excluding Islam from political life that Islamism has now acquired the image of "a value which is persecuted, and consequently a revolutionary force". In other words, the Islamic elan of the masses will become all the more revolutionary if they feel that Islam is being suppressed and persecuted.

The writer nowhere names Col. Muʿammar al-Qadhdhāfī, although he does single out post-revolutionary Libya as the only Arab state that has dared to pronounce itself for Islam.[4] In any case, it is clear that in advocating the use of Islam as a revolutionary force he is taking a position similar to that of the Libyan revolutionary leader. On more than one occasion, al-Qadhdhāfī has been known to bypass the authorities in other Arab countries in order to address himself to the Islamic sentiments of their subjects. And, during last summer's debate on sectarian discrimination on the part of the Lebanese government, it was al-Qadhdhāfī who told the Lebanese Muslims that they were third-class citizens, after the Maronites and the Greek Orthodox. The writer of the two replies, ʿUthman ʿUthman, also understands the article as a defence of the Libyan position on the role of Islam in the Arab revolution, since he is at pains to point out that a policy which may be good for Libya, which is 100% Muslim, may not be so good for other Arab countries which are less homogeneous religiously. See also his warning against "the renewal of confessional trading under the guise of Nasserism" at the end of his second reply.

About the authors: Munaḥ Solḥ is a member of an old Beirut Sunni Muslim family which has given to Lebanese political life such well-known personalities as Riyad al-Solḥ the first Premier of the Republic, and Taqi al-Din al-Solḥ, the present Premier, who is the uncle of the writer. Munaḥ Solḥ attented International College in Beirut, the Maqāsid secondary school in the same city, and has made some studies at the Sorbonne. He has contributed articles on political and social subjects to such reviews as al-Mawāqif, al-Thaqafah al-ᶜArabiyah, and the Sunday supplement of al-Nahar. He is commonly identified with leftist and progressive causes, although in leftist circles he is regarded as quite moderate.

ᶜUthman ᶜUthman is a young Arab (Syrian) writer.

Notes:

1. CEMAM Reports, I (Beirut: 1973), N°1 pp. 159-197
2. See below, p. 13.
3. See below, p. 15.
4. See below, p. 4.

THE ARABISM OF THE AVANT GARDE

AND THE ISLAMISM OF THE MASSES +

by MUNAḤ SOLḤ

translated by SHEREEN KHAIRALLAH

Immediately after 5 June[1], a royal government in the Arab Maghrib said that the underlying reason for that defeat was the forgetfulness of the 'umma of its traditions and spiitual values. It was to be expected that rulers of the Maghrib would adhere to Islam and its politics, were it only as an additional weapon in the war against progressives (whom their government accuses of being unbelievers). But what is happening today in the Maghrib causes amazement: the ruler, who is the prince of believers (amīr al-mu'minīn), scarcely talks about Islam; he limits his words to one thing: the struggle between Berber and non-Berber.

Revolutions have taken place, demonstrations have occurred, and the government has not said one word concerning the lack of Islam among the rebels, the opposition, and the revolutionaries. That is because popular resentment against the ruler is stronger than the help these words would give. His need is for ethnic fragmentation, tribal fragmentation, and regional fragmentation, while Islam in this case would unite, it would not divide. That is why he brings up the subject of Berber and non-Berber, and closes the door on the subject of Islam.

In Libya, al-Sanūsi[2] did not dare talk about Islam, in spite of the fact of his being an Imam, for his policy was isolation, and to speak about Islam would mean his coming out of isolation. Libya had to revolt against al-Sanūsi, and the first of September[3] had to come before the Libyan government would dare to pronounce itself for Islam. And this is in spite of the fact that the Islam of the Libyan system does not exactly represent the progressive face of Islam; and if it spoke of Islam after June [4], it would logically have felt compelled to come out of isolation and bring Libya into the Arab bloc.

As for Tunis, she protects her ties with the West by accusing Islam of negativism and backwardness, according to the official line.

Algeria comes closer to Islam, but only to the extent of approaching a policy of Arabization and support of Palestine, no more, no less.

+ from al-Islam wa ḥarakat ul-taḥarrur al-arabī (Islam and the Arab Liberation movement), Beirut (1973), pp. 50-68.

And in the Mashriq (East), even the princes of the Arabian Peninsula keep silent on Islamic policy, in as much as a ruler can, in that area, keep quiet about Islam.

In Jordan the talk is about Jordanianism and Palestinianism, while mention of Islam lessens, for fear that it would favor solidarity and defiance.

The stand of the Arab progressive governments towards Islam is that of a current Arab progressive stand; it is the position which dreads any discussion of Islam in politics, generally speaking, and says that its dangers are greater than its benefits.

Thus, in enumerating the positions of the Arab nations towards Islam, we see that, for one reason or another, these nations, especially the reactionaries among them, tend to be breaking away from the use of Islam as a means.

This breaking away puts us in a new position; it allows us, from the start of the Arab liberation movement, to be open to the Islamism of the masses, in order to build up, in the face of imperialism and zionism, such a true popular revolutionary movement, a movement with such deep roots, as to enable it to have the power to face the West which is creeping into our country, -- the political, economic and social West, the civilized and cultural West.

DISTINCTIONS AND INTERACTIONS BETWEEN ARABISM AND ISLAM

The Arab nationalist movement was born in the shadow of a living historical necessity, with preference for an Arab nationalist tie rather than an Ottoman religious tie.

For the Turkish nationalist consciousness pursued a policy of mastery over the Arab nationalist consciousness, with Islam and the protection of the nation of the Caliphate as an excuse.

From the beginning, therefore, the Arab nationalist movement had to be sensitive in its understanding of the distinctive characteristics of both the nationalist tie and the religious tie.

This, in fact, took place. Perhaps this historical necessity assured it a safe birth, which was not granted to some other national movements. Because of the ambiguity of the non-nationalist religious tie, the Arab nationalist movement was born at an early period and was nursed on its path of national liberation by armed conflict with other Islamic nations.

From the first days, the problem of the relationship between religion and nationalism was tied to a great extent to the Arab nationalist movement.

But the intellectual and political circles continued to reject the idea that this distinction came about, not from a desire to protect nationalist thought from reactionary religious domination, but rather from a desire to keep Islam outside the revolution.

For they say that this distinction between Arabism and Islam did not happen for the sake of saying: there is incompatibility between them.

And these circles insist that there is a problem of making a distinction between Arabism and Islamism. They dread, consciously or unconsciously, the claim of interaction between these two distinct truths. They are afraid of the results of the revolutionary leap in Arabism and Islam, and in the Arab liberation movement, once this interaction is accomplished.

It is as though they desire to hand out shares, giving the label of "reaction" to Islam while the progressives, its enemies, take the rest.

The time has passed, after the breakdown of the union between Egypt and Syria, in which certain reactionary classes almost created in some Arab countries a synonymity between the word Muslim, when used in a political speech, and their interests as a class. For the individual would identify himself as a Muslim in order to say he is against nationalization, for instance, or against socialism or progressive parties.

But this situation only remained for a particular period and disappeared shortly after the Israeli occupation. The word Muslim has been stripped, in the mind of every individual, of all reactionary meanings associated with it, and its anti-imperialist and anti-zionist luster has returned to it. It is related that one of the officials in the Arab Socialist Union (Egypt) said: we may lose Sinai, we won't lose our Muslim faith.

However, the very notoriety which this statement received points to its incompatibility with the people's understanding of the deep union between this faith and the liberation of Sinai.

Thus, when the Arab masses speak of their Islam in the form of a political or cultural position, most of the time they mean to confirm their refusal of subordination to the West, to confirm that they historically and geographically are part of a whole, that they possess a heritage, values, and roots.

In short, they signify the same group of principles which the avant-garde originators of Arabism and the Arab liberation movement exalt.

The difference concerns the clarity of the vision of reality and the ability to express it, not at all the depth of attachment to the national and human truth.

Sometimes there is in the proclamation by the masses of their Islam a positive tenacity on their part, so that they say to the cultured, Westernized and pretentious avant-garde: I am from one world and you are from another, I am different from you; they mean that they surpass this group in their being in (rather than out of) harmony with the national character.

Perhaps the masses in their Islam live more truly in accord with Arab goals and are more prepared to give themselves for those goals than do some of the cultured proponents of nationlist principles.

ISLAM: THE ARABISM OF THE MAGHRIB

Even in special cases, where certain segments of the Muslim masses (e.g., some Berbers in North Africa) move to the point of denying their Arab identity, Arabization, in the sense we mentioned earlier, remains an artificial duty.

For the native of the Maghrib in saying "I am not an Arab but a Berber", does not mean that he is attempting to get out of an obligation which we in the East connect in our mind with the word Arabism, as pride in the Arab heritage, solidarity with Arab regions, looking towards unity, and confidence in the capabilities, aims, and national role; all these obligations the Arab of the Maghrib feels within himself by the mere fact that he is a Muslim; Islam for him is what Arabism is for us - in addition, of course, to the purely religious aspect.

But to him the word "Arab", which he rejects, has no more than a clannish, tribal or regional connotation with which he has no connection.

The sum of the values and ties which move us in the Mashriq and which we consider as Arabism, is what moves the Arab or the Berber and what they consider Islam.

We must not fall into the trap of imperialism and imagine that the denial of the word Arab in certain circles of the Maghrib is a denial of what is contained in the word Arabism nor a refusal of the brotherhood and the truth of the two nationalisms.

It is wrong for us to compare the role of Islam in the Maghrib with its role in bringing together, for instance, the two nationalisms, Arab nationalism and Kurdish nationalism , in Iraq.

For Islam in North Africa is not a factor of rapprochement between two nationalisms. Not only is it another name for Arab nationalism, but more correctly, it is the name used in the Maghrib for what we mean by national ties.

A declaration there of membership in Islam by the Berber or by the Arab is an expression of belief in a common nationalism, a nationalism uniting the two of them, on the one hand, and uniting them and every other Arab, on the other.

In fact, the case of the Maghrib, from this point of view, is an extreme one: Islam there means Arabism, but this is not exactly the case of Arab countries in other regions. But the resemblance at present remains.

ISLAMISM OF THE MASSES AND ARABISM OF THE AVANT-GARDE

In talking about Islam, the masses everywhere mean the allegiance to the basic sides of the national issue.

The reactionary imperialistic conspiracy focuses on the following: the illusion of the avant-garde that the Islam of the masses is basically different from the Arabism of the avant-garde, and the illusion of the masses that the Arabism of the avant-garde is basically different from the Islam of the masses.

Thus it is easy for imperialism to work positively and negatively with that type of Arabism of the intellectuals which is far removed from the heritage and the masses, and with that type of Islam which is far removed from the centre of the national call.

Both of these are in agreement with the interests of a cosmopolitanism which forms the philosophy of the imperialistic cultural incursion into this area.

The "pure" national appeal which thrives in the intellectual milieu, is an appeal to build a modern society after the pattern of Western societies, in the hope of extending Western life to the East. Although this appeal may have met resistance from imperialism, imperialism did not see in it a dangerous enemy; and many of imperialism's universities in our country were the cradle of this appeal.

The same thing may be said for the Islamism which does not directly join the national cause. Imperialism has not taken its cautious and suspicious eye off this trend for one day, nor opposed it by force but rather has often encouraged some of its personalities. What contented imperialism was, in the first place, the ease of inciting this trend along the road to false progress, and, secondly, the ease of convincing it (this trend) to be content with backwardness.

The main aim of imperialism was, with the passage of days, to provoke those dubious imprecations in the name of religion which intensified against every movement for change, and which became tolerant of the imperialist because of the deficiency in nationalist solidarity.

TWO VIEWS ON ISLAM

Imperialism spent much effort in creating a specific point of view, among the Arab citizen and the world as a whole, towardsIslam. For imperialism sets out from the idea that Islam is a basic force and an active presence in Arab life, and likewise, from its knowledge that its (imperialism's) entry into Arab life is tied to a great extent to the view which Arabs have, both Muslims and non-Muslims, towards Islam.

Imperialism does not stop at the formation of the view of the Arab Muslim towards Islam, but goes on to the view of every Arab towards Islam. Imperialism understands that the relationship between Islam and Arab nationalism is not, for instance, like the relationship between Catholicism and French nationalism, or Protestantism and the U.S.A. or Orthodoxy and Greece.

Imperialism also understands that the connection between Islam and Arab nationalism is not the same as that between Islam and Iranian nationalism, for example, or even between Islam and Turkish nationalism. This is because the Arab _'umma_ was formed and entered its historical stage and fashioned Islam, just as Islam was born and reached its peak while fashioning the Arab 'umma; thus there is no possibility for the forged, arbitrary and specious distinction between the life of Islam and the life of the Arab 'umma, neither in the past, nor in the present, nor in the future.

Islam by its heritage, values, and concepts makes up the greater part of the national culture of any Arab, whether he be Muslim or non-Muslim. On these grounds, cultural imperialism , in its dealings with the Arab personality and in its attempt to influence it, must, of necessity, work with the Arab view towards Islam.

How does cultural imperialism wish us to look at Islam ?

On this subject, cultural imperialism wishes us to have one of two viewpoints, which, in appearance, are far apart and contradictory, but in the end serve the same purpose.

The first view varies between considering Islam as the cause of backwardness in the life of the Arabs and sometimes in the life of the world, and considering Islam as a religion like any other religion; in the life of Arabs, it is just like other religions in the life of the rest of the nations.

This mistaken view of Islam in its different shapes and forms gets the strong encouragement of imperialism, which very well knows that change in Arab life will not be radical, if its roots are cut off from a specific domestic, national, and spiritual heritage. Imperialism knows that Westernization is one thing and revolution another. Thus we see imperialism being positive, and even more than positive, towards the renascence movements in the East and in Arab countries, and to a certain extent imperialism took this negative view of Islam.

The two greatest examples of this are Kamalism in Turkey and Bourguibism in Tunisia. These two movements met with an understanding from the West and an approval and support which passed all limits. The reason is that these two movements embrace shame for the Islamic heritage and for its connection with the East. They both have an eye on the credentials of European life in all its phases, and they dream of the possibility of transporting this civilization and planting it in the East. This puts the Western imperialist at ease, for it makes the relationship between himself and the developing nation one of borrowing and imitation, not one of interaction through the operations of taking and resisting.

Imperialism has succeeded in convincing some "intellectual revolutionaries" that the revolution in Arab life begins by creating a revolution against the slogans of Islam and its rites, for the revolution enters Arab life just as the Lord Jesus says of the entry of a rich man into heaven,i.e., through the eye of a needle. For in the logic of these people the revolutionary should begin his work by announcing his atheism or his non-Islamism; at least then he can face the rest of his revolutionary tasks. He must demand of the citizen the certificate of his atheism and non-faith in Islam in order to enroll him in the ranks of the revolution.

Such a widespread view among innocent intellectuals is the

biggest plot against the revolutionary cause, because nothing is better for reactionism than the following equation: the revolution is atheism, and reactionism is religion ! Is not atheism, from the practical point of view, at least, the weakest point in the revolution, and religion the strongest in reaction ? The mature revolution, the victorious revolution, focusing on economic and social achievements, substituting just human relations for those of exploitation, this revolution, after reaching a high degree of stability, is the only one that can expose the religious issues and allow individual stands, whatever they may be.

But to say to a young revolution which is just starting, or which scarcely exists, as is the case in most Arab regions: it is your duty to take a stand towards religion as a basic measure of your "revolutionariness", means asking the revolution to bury itself at the beginning of its road.

This does not mean, in any case, that the revolutionary should not have complete clarity on the subject of preventing the use of religion for reactionary and imperialistic purposes. It also does not mean that the revolutionary should not have a clear idea of what real religion is, the religion which is conviction, the religion which is the spiritual source. Nor does it mean that the revolutionary should not have a deep and full respect for the freedom of each individual to believe or not to believe. On the contrary, the revolutionary would not be a revolutionary if he did not have all these prerequisites.

The second dangerous view, which imperialism wishes to implant through Orientalist schools, or, to be exact, some of them, is the sanctification of institutions of the past, and the surrounding of these institutions with haloes of perfection and imagining them, especially in their petrified forms in the ages of decline, as being the ultimate style of life and the only one which agrees with the Arab mind, Arab competence, and Arab conditions, and that Arabs have no choice but to return to it if they want success, that they should return to it as it is literally and formally, and to all that is frozen in it, not to its spirit and its thought and the origin of its growth.

It is not exceptional to find Arabs educated in the big European or American universities who return to their country with the highest degrees to preach to the sons of their _'umma_ the perfection of all that is past, and all that has collapsed with time, giving these opinions in the face of the methodology of modern political science and, in the face of the new forces, nay, in the face of the inclination to change, simple and free of all complexes, which is found in each citizen.

Cultural imperialism has achieved two successes: the intellectual who believes there is no road to progress except on the rubble of Islam, and the intellectual who believes there is no road to progress except through a return to past institutions, with the idea that this is Islam and there is no other Islam but this.

The first method succeeds among intellectuals, and "revolutionaries" and the reformist parties. The second method exists among academicians and university professors and the sons of the rich, who lead lives of the extreme luxury found in the West.

But neither of the two can in any way convince the masses,

the common man. For the people are still untouched by this point of view, and on the one hand are not at ease with this articial type of revolutionary who wants to strike them in their heritage before presenting them with material achievements or calling them to a tangible national or social battle. On the other hand they are not at ease with the comfortable Westernized man who lives a totally Western life, then calls them to return to past institutions and a style of life without alteration or change.

The only way to break loose from coercion of the objective and implicit alliance between the view rejecting religion and the rigid view towards religion is by understanding the role which religion plays in each phase of historical evolution.

Today, more than any day past, and more especially following the Palestine defeat, it is clear that Islam is in the ranks of the revolution, not elsewhere. The Arab liberation movement is in need of a mental and organizational leap, a leap in spiritual courage, to evaluate the form of its primary, moral, and permanent relationship with Islam.

ISLAM IN THE RANKS OF THE REVOLUTION

An Arab liberation movement unaffected by the vestiges of Western complexes towards Islam has the qualifications to understand this role, and to deal with the effects of the abovementioned alliance on the advancement of freedom and progress in the Arab nation and to move towards national goals with all the force of the masses.

For the continued presence of complexes towards Islam among some of these intellectuals engaged in national action will obstruct a clear view and delay free and complete interaction with the masses, and will deny the Arab liberation movement the inspiration of their authentic nature and their intellectual beliefs which bespeak an absolute positiveness with regard to Islam as a legacy and as a religion.

At present, Islam lives in a phase emancipated from the domination of imperialism and reaction. National chauvinism and ethnic tendencies are today the dominant characteristics of the regimes of non-Arab Islamic nations, who avoid solidarity with the Arabs in the battle of Palestine, who are pressured by international imperialistic powers to entangle themselves in artificially created fights with the Arabs. This evasion and entanglement have put them in a position of fearing to mount Islamic slogans which for a long time they had used as mottos for their internal and foreign politics.

And the same goes for the Arab countries, where regionalisms and provincialisms are too strong to allow them to get closer to Islam, and to try to use it strongly in politics.

Whoever looks at these facts from a reactionary point of view finds that Islam is being defeated, and that Eastern and Arab regimes are abandoning, generally speaking, the policy of Islamic alliances and appearances, but those who look at the situation from the point of view of the Arab liberation movement see, on the contrary, that Islam, after its relative liberation from imperialistic and reactionary domination, has become, as its essence imposes, the natural and strong support of the Arab liberation movement.

For Islam has remained a possession of the masses, and to the extent that we understand their Islamism, and to the extent that we revolt against the cold, haughty, sick culture of the poisoned intellectuals, to the same extent we can join in pushing our <u>'umma</u> into the progressive age with all the power of the masses.

There is no one who thinks of Islam, in our time, in any country, but that he feels he faces a value which is persecuted, and consequently a revolutionary force.

This is what makes Islam the historical twin of the Arab liberation movement.

The chimerical problem of some of the intellectuals is that the masses are Muslim and consequently their Arabism has not yet been finalized. At this time there is nothing in fact which justifies saying that a lack in the Arabism of the masses is a function of a superabundance of their Islamism.

The phenomenon of a lack in Arabism is not usually found where Islam abounds, but where reaction, regionalism, <u>shu^{c}ūbiyya</u>,[5] cosmopolitanism, or other such manifestations are found.

Generally speaking, it is wrong to think of danger to Arabism as coming from Islam, which comes to fill the place of Arabism.

The measure for defining the stand in this issue is: Does the Islamism of the masses create a burden on the Arab national movement, or is it an additional dimension of it ?

The question here is directed at the leftists, westernized in thought, and at the rightists (motivated by personal) interests, who are united in their insistence on keeping Islam outside the revolution.

Editor's Notes

1. The June war of 1967
2. King Idris
3. The day of the revolution led by Col. Qadhdhafi.
4. The June war of 1967
5 It is difficult to find an exact equivalent for this word. It indicates, basically, non-Arabism or internationalism. See Hanna and Gardner, <u>Arab Socialism</u> (Brill, 1969) p.80 ff.

ANSWER TO MUNAḤ SOLḤ'S ARTICLE ON "THE ARABISM OF THE AVANT-GARDE AND THE ISLAMISM OF THE MASSES"+

by ᶜUTHMAN ᶜUTHMAN

In his article "The Arabism of the avant-garde and the Islamism of the masses", Munah Solḥ brought up the subject of the relationship between the Arab revolution and Islam. He ended his article with a norm; he said that it is the decisive rule: "Does Islam form a burden on the Arab revolutionary movement?"

This norm set by Mr. Solḥ, or imagined by him, is at the same time a question, a general, comprehensive, foggy question, and not one limited in scope and horizon, not a scientific question. First, what Mr. Solḥ regards as a norm, is not a norm. Then, Munaḥ al-Solḥ sometimes talks about the spirituality of Islam, and sometimes about the traditions of Islam which have been established over the course of thirteen centuries.

What Mr. Solḥ feels are the traditions and history of Islam, is Islamic political applications and data. And politics, as all know, are the behaviour of the governing power and the ethics of the governing power, and both of these are affected by the needs of every age, every generation, and every period of human development.

Religion is the relation between man and his God, whereas the policy of a nation is the connection between rule, the governing power, and the governed, and between the governing power and other nations and regimes.

BATTLE BETWEEN TWO FACTIONS

The Battle of Siffīn is between two factions of Muslims, each faction, and the soldiers of each, believing in the doctrine of monotheism. But each of these two factions fought for political power to defeat the enemy. So, religion is one, there is a difference over political power, and the victims are 50,000 or more.

Then there is the Battle of the Camel, and its victims were equal to those of the Battle of Siffīn. Which traditions

+ from Muharrir 31/7/73, p.11

does Mr. Solh want us to adopt ? The traditions of Muʿāwiya's politics, or those of ʿAlī, the martyr ʿAlī ?

I personally am not of the Shīʿā confession, and I refuse the national division before refusing the confessional division for one religious creed. However, because the documents of history confirm that ʿAlī ibn Abī Ṭālib was the first to believe in the Muhammadan call, and that Muʿāwiya became Muslim the day of the conquest of Mecca - and this historical fact has great significance - I would have liked the victory to go to the martyr ʿAlī.

The Battle of Siffīn was the beginning of political exploitation of Islam as a doctrine of monotheism, and as a political power, and as economic interests.

In the Battle of Siffīn Muʿāwiya realized a military victory, then a political one, against the most firm believer in the Muhammadan call.

And in the Battle of the Camel, ʿAisha lost the military and political battle, despite the fact that she, since her marriage with the Prophet, had great religious faith.

The Battle of Siffīn, and after it the Battle of the Camel, made certain a very important truth, and that is the necessity of the division between politics and religion, between military wars and religion, between the building of a political nation and the doctrine of monotheism.

When we do not admit to this documented historical truth, we confirm, without being aware of it, that political opportunism, and trafficking in the religious call, are the way to build nations, and the path to transient military victory.

The Prophet Muhammad united political power and the doctrine of monotheism. This is true. Then the Orthodox Caliphs came after him and continued this procedure, and innovated and perfected the aims of the Prophet Muhammad. But the Orthodox Caliphs ended with the military victory of Muʿāwiya over ʿAli. Thus, with the end of the Orthodox Caliphs the necessity of making a division between Islam as a spiritual issue and Islam as a political issue was ascertained.

When a Prophet like Muḥammad comes to mankind, then the controversial tie between politics and religion will return, between the building of the nation and the mission of Islam. But the Qur'ān says that Muhammad is the last prophet. Then hope is ended for the union of politics and religion. The Orthodox Caliphs learned at the hand of Muhammad personally, and were influenced by his indifference to power. And Muʿāwiya did not personally learn at the hand of the Prophet. Muʿāwiya was the last to believe the Muhammadan call, he believed the day of the conquest of Mecca, when there was no way but for him to declare his submission (Islam).

NATIONAL REVOLUTIONARY MOVEMENT

The Arab revolution is a political national revolutionary movement. It is a political movement because it is directed towards the building of an Arab nation which brings together Arab groups of different religious faiths. And it is a political movement clashing with the politics of the Zionist American enemy, and with the Arab powers which are politically, economically, and militarily allied with the Zionist American enemy. The Arab revolution, this being its orientation, cannot adopt Islam in the sense of political traditions which have become rooted over the period of twelve centuries after the Orthodox Caliphs. The Arab revolution can only make certain of the division between politics and religion, between the building of the nation and the religious mission of Islam, and also of Christianity. This division was not invented by the Arab revolution, neither by Orientalists nor by imperialists, as Mr. Solḥ says, and as the Lebanese and the Muslim Brothers imagine. This division was ascertained by Muᶜāwiya at Siffīn.

RESPONSIBILITIES OF THE ARAB REVOLUTION

The Arab revolution faces extremely complicated circumstances on two levels, national and international. Thus it faces extremely complicated international politics, and international changes too. The point on which the Arab revolutionary movement hinges is the defeat of the Zionist American enemy and the building of a united Arab nation from the Atlantic to the Gulf. This is the target, which meets many difficulties and which asks martyrdom from all the nationalist fighters, regardless of their religious affiliation, for the sake of surmounting its difficulties. Because the Arab revolution does not want another Siffīn and a second Battle of the Camel, and because it does not want a new Mongol domination, nor a new Turkish domination, it refuses to adopt the Islamic political traditions, it refuses to mix politics and religion.

But on the other hand, the Arab revolution is proud of Islam as a doctrine of monotheism, as a spiritual cause. It is proud of the memory of the Prophet Muḥammad, and of his mission, and of his genius, and of his prophethood. It is proud of the memory of the Orthodox Caliphs because they were charged with the directives of the Prophet Muḥammad, and because they were his contemporaries and took some of his characteristics.

The Arab revolution must also be proud of the spiritual mission of Christianity. Because the Prophet Muḥammad made clear his respect for the followers of this mission (of monotheism), and did not detest them for their religion or look down on them.

The Arab revolution when it refuses the union of politics and the spiritual mission, does so because it does not want to make it possible for any new Muᶜāwiya to accomplish his opportunistic (designs) at the expense of the 'umma under the veil of a religious call.

The Arab revolution does not adopt a new religious mission, because, basically, it does not believe in the mixing of politics and the religious message. But the Arab revolution will protect the beliefs of all present religious sects. It will not allow one religious sect to oppress another. From this viewpoint, the Arab revolution announces its absolute protection of the religious message of each sect of the one doctrine, and also to the doctrines opposing some of the above. No confessional oppression, no oppression by minorities of the nationalist minorities which are brothers with the Arab nationalists. Is not this duty noble and splendid ?

THE PECULIARITY OF THE LIBYAN POSITION

Libya is distinguished by an important characteristic, that is, that 100% of its population belong to Islam, and, moreover, it adheres to the same doctrine and rite of Islam.

But this characteristic is found nowhere else but in Libya. So that, although we supposed, for the sake of argument, that the Arab revolution would adopt the Islamic program, even in a vague way: religion plus politics, what will this revolution adopt ? The traditions of which political age ? The Umayyad traditions ? Or the ᶜAbbasid traditions ? Or the Turkish traditions ? Or the Fatimid traditions ? Or the Sanūsī traditions ? Or the Wahhabī traditions ? Or the Saffarid traditions ? Or the Andalusian traditions ? Or the Khārijite traditions ? These sects have been sanctified for twelve centuries. So how do we create a single unity in this present historical phase ?

Then all these sects, besides the Christian sects, have an interest in bringing an end to the inimical Zionist American presence.

The enemy does not differentiate between a Muslim and a non-Muslim, between one sect and another. The enemy is not aiming at changing Muslims and non-Muslims into Jews, but the enemy is aiming at ruining the potentialities of the 'umma, regardless of the religious affiliation of those potentialities. The enemy has accomplished much of this aim up to now. And the enemy by this aim, in alliance with American imperialism, wishes to rob the Arab world of its wealth.

The enmity therefore is not religious. It is political and military and economic, a national enmity. And opposition to it must be national.

Why did not all the potentialities of the Arab 'umma share in resisting this racist aggression ? How is resistance with all the potentialities of the 'umma possible when some desire the division within the ranks of the 'umma, and the setting of one doctrine above another ? Then in one doctrine there are different sects. So how is it possible to unite the ranks within one doctrine, and with the domination of one doctrinal sect over others? Hence, the Arab revolution has decided its stand:

Yes to brotherhood between Islam and Christianity.

No to the mixing of politics and religion.

Yes to respect for all religious rituals for each sect of each doctrine.

No to sectarian persecution.

Nationalism makes brothers and unites the ranks, it does not divide.

Nationalism is a message of brotherhood among all religious affiliations in the Arab 'umma, and it - nationalism - announces its brotherhood with the national minorities found on the soil of the fatherland.

Glory to nationalism. And priority and only priority to the defeat of the Zionist and American aggressions. And glory to the martyrs of the Arab national revolution.

ANSWER TO MUNAḤ SOLḤ'S ARTICLE ON "THE ARABISM OF THE AVANT-GARDE AND THE ISLAMISM OF THE MASSES"+

by ᶜUTHMAN ᶜUTHMAN

Munaḥ al-Solḥ made a serious political and historical mistake when he said that Islam "created" the Arab 'umma.

Islam is a religious message and called for better relations among mankind.

With Islam, no human being came down from heaven. Islam came to preach to nations, and the Arab 'umma is the first nation Islam addressed.

Islam began on Arab soil.

Islam began in the Arab 'umma.

The language of the Qur'ān was Arabic.

The denial of the presence of the 'umma before the appearance of Islam was the pit into which fell the Muslim Brothers and the Nabhāniyyuh [1].

The denial of the political right of the Arab 'umma to an independent nation is the spark which lit the beginning of the revolution between the Arab avant-garde and the Turks.

Political right is one thing, and religious belief another. They differ in both essence and in aim.

There is no difference between the belief of an Arab in Islam as a monotheistic doctrine and between the belief of a Turk or an Iranian in this doctrine. But, that the Turk insist on exercising political tutelage and on being a political governor over the Arab, is a different proposition.

Tribal consciousness is one thing, and consciousness of membership in the Arab 'umma another. Religious affiliation is a bond between man and his God. The national tie is a bond between human groups joined together by shared characteristics, the most important of which are one language, a common history, common economic interests, common hopes and sufferings. Sometimes religious affiliation is one of these characteristics.

Tribal bigotry is rejected within the nation itself, because it is the antithesis of national political unity.

+ from Muharrir 1/8/73, pp. 9,11

THE TASK OF ISLAM

The basic task of the Muhammadan call is to spread the doctrine of monotheism on the ruins of paganism.

The task of the Prophet Muḥammad was not to submit the Islamic nations to one governor.

For the ruler is a means, not an end; and government is a means not a goal in itself.

At the appearance of the Muhammadan call, war was the means to propagate the call, it was the only means. There was no printing. War took the place of the information media.

In order to make it possible for the Prophet Muḥammad to fulfill his mission of (spreading) monotheism, it was necessary for him to raise a nation, and to enable the army of this nation to spread the monotheistic message.

And in as much as government is the means of propagating the call, and war the means of making it reach other nations, then the presence of other means, alternate and helpful, abolishes war and political power as a means of propagating the religious call.

The connection between one ruler for the Islamic nations and "the doctrine of monotheism" is what encouraged the absolution of the tyrants among the Caliphs and the flourishing of the age of concubinage and slavery. As long as religious faith, faith in the spirituality of Islam, was not brought about by force, how can the governed of different nations be forced to obey one ruler ?

THE DOCTRINE OF MONOTHEISM

So that the caliphs - after the Orthodox Caliphs - could justify the extension of their political authority over large parts of the civilized world, and over all nations which believed in the Islamic doctrine of monotheism, there was no way but to justify this world political domination, and these sultans had no choice but to bring out fatwas to crush the political independence of nations. The mission of monotheism was the first task of the Prophet Muḥammad. For instance, that monotheism is clear from the first Qur'anic verse, whereas the later verses are either to present more proofs of monotheism, or to face the unforeseen relations of the governed amongst each other, or in their relations with the authority.

Another proof, also, of the correctness of our point of view, is that the Prophet Muḥammad did not draw up any clear, established manner for succession. The lack of any established mode for (resolving) this problem, was the gap through which Mu^{c}āwiya made his entrance, and was the justification for the Battle of the Camel and other political struggles for power.

But the political leadership for the Prophet, besides his prophethood, fortified the Prophet Muḥammad for admirable success in building the foundation of the Arab state, inspired by his monotheistic mission. The Prophet Muḥammad was concerned with the propagation of this mission, the doctrine of monotheism, among the tribes of the Arab 'umma first, and secondly among other nations. To achieve this goal, the existence of a state was necessary because the Arab 'umma was divided and occupied by the Persians and Romans.

In order that the state be centralized and its domination be established over the tribes, who clung to their spirit of tribal independence, it was necessary to establish the domination of the central authority. Hence, the justification of the glorious verse: "Obey God and the Prophet and those in authority among you" (Sura IV: 59).

Since there is no compulsion in religion, with all the more reason there should be no compulsion in political submission. But in the stage (of civilization) contemporaneous with the Muhammadan call, the sole means for spreading the doctrine of monotheism was by military battles; and the building of the centralized Arab state was to insure this strong army, this only means of information in that age.

NO TIES BETWEEN POLITICAL AUTHORITY AND RELIGIOUS FAITH

From this truth, that there exist means of information other than armies and battles and nation-building, it follows that these means so closely associated (with the beginnings of the mission) should be dropped when there are alternate means.

In other words, when the union of all Arab groups was achieved within the Arab state, and when after a period of time the proclamation of the doctrine of monotheism to all the Arab masses was assured and those who wished submitted to Islam and those who did not submit remained with their own doctrine - this was their right according to the precepts of the Islamic call - then the tie of political power to religious faith became unnecessary. This was what was confirmed at the Battle of Siffīn.

At the Battle of Siffīn, when the Arab 'umma had assured the political unity of most of the Arab lands, the division between politics and religion was confirmed - by documents and by blood also. ᶜAlī, in the Battle of Siffīn, represented the continuation of the Orthodox Caliphs, those geniuses, extraordinary in their fusion of political power with the mission of monotheism. Muᶜawiya represented political opportunism and trafficking in the religious call. And if Muᶜāwiya accomplished a military and political victory over the most hardened fighters of the Islamic mission, this is what confirmed the necessity of separating political power from the doctrine of monotheism. al-Tabarī relates on the authority of al-Hasan al-Basirī:

'Umar ibn al-Khattab had forbidden the prominent Quraish from leaving the country without permission.

al-Shaᶜbī said: "'Umar did not die until the Quraish got tired of him. He had blocked them in the city and had said: the thing I fear most for this 'umma is your dispersion in the lands". And al-Shaᶜbī also said: "When 'Uthman freed the Quraish they became a cause of unrest in the land and people began making their way to them".

al-Tabarī recounts, with his authorities: "Not a year of 'Uthman's emirate had passed before some men from the Quraish took money from the military centers and people began frequenting them".

So that the Quraish aristocracy could exploit the situations of the new state, the Arab state, and the situation of other Muslim nations, they had to exploit politically the mission of monotheism, and to confirm the "internationality" of Islam, the internationality of the political power, the political unity of one political Islamic state containing different nations.

Thus, in order that the privileges of the aristocratic class of the Quraish be established, they set about establishing the centralization of political power in the Islamic state over all Islamic nations. When this political program was assured, dominion was for the Quraish. So the centralization of political power for the one Islamic state, and the denial of national political independence, were the road to ensuring the political suzerainty of the Quraish over this state.

And when the Mongols came, and the Turks after them, they used the very same arguments as the Quraish - political unity for one Islamic state - and negated nationalism. Thus, the philosophy of the internationalism of Islam politically, the unity of political power, was the seed which made others besides the Arabs rule over the Arabs and debase them, spreading poverty and illness and rape and terror.

NATIONAL AFFILIATION

The negation of national affiliation along with the desire to mix politics and religion were the political entree for the invasion by the Mongols and then the Turks of the Arab nation and for the monopolization of political tutelage and political protection over the Arab 'umma.

"No difference between white and black", "no distinction of Arab over non-Arab" means no national superiority, but does not deny national affiliation. It means that the message of monotheism is for the white and the black, for the Arab and the non-Arab, and these words do not at all mean the submission of the Iranian nation to the dominion of the Quraish, nor the submission of the Arab 'umma to the Iranians and Turks.

The message of monotheism is one thing, and political domination of one nation over another, something else. This means that the message of monotheism is one thing and the national question, as a political problem, is another. Because 'Umar (al-Fārūq) realized the ambitions of the Quraish for political trading with the Muhammadan call, and owing to this realization alone, he was the first to suppress the political freedom of one class, the forced residence of the Quraish in Mecca.

The tyrannical Turkish authority over the Arab 'umma clashes with the idea of Arab nationalism; for that reason the task of the Turkish authority was to prepare hangings for the propagators of nationalism, even though the propagators of national thought did not ask the Arab masses to forego the Islamic doctrine of monotheism, nor to forego Christianity.

THE DECISION

The Arab revolution has decided its position vis-à-vis the national problem, once and for all. The mere fact that the Arab revolution stands on its own feet is a certain indication of its national political principle. In like manner, the Arab revolution has decided its position, definitively, vis-à-vis the problem of the political aspirations of the doctrine of monotheism, and of those who traffic in that doctrine.

cAbd al-Nasir announced the above two inseparable stands the morning of the hangings. In the name of the Arab 'umma, and in the name of the Arab revolution, to the traders in confessionalism in Egypt, cAbd al-Nasir did not hang the doctrine of monotheism in Egypt the day he hanged the Muslim Brothers. On the contrary he brought out the death sentence in the name of the 'umma and the Arab revolution against those who tried to exploit the doctrine of monotheism on the political level, and against those who insisted on ignoring the political right of the Arab 'umma, those who want to oppose the national movement.

In cAbd al-Nasir's stand is courage in facing the battle, courage while facing the traders in confessionalism -- no matter the colour and sect of the trade -- for he did not want new divisions within the 'umma, nor persecution of one confession by another, nor persecution of one sect by another.

ALL ARE FACING THE ENEMY

We face a vicious foe and a vicious ally of our foe. We face the Zionist American enemy. In order that the resistance to the enemy be successful and solid, it is necessary that all potentialities of the 'umma share in this courageous resistance, all the sects of all the doctrines of the 'umma. There is no superiority of one doctrine over another, nor of one sect over another.

The Arab revolution will never allow any problem to override the problem of the unified liberation struggle, the problem of the national revolutionary struggle against the enemies of national existence.

The view of the Arab revolution towards the traders in confessional problems is the view of cAbd al-Nasir to this suspect commerce which impedes the national struggle.

cAbd al-Nasir did not give an opinion, but asserted an attitude and pronounced a judgement.

With regard to the renewal of confessional trading under the veil of Nasirism, this is the new game and the new conspiracy.

In front of this dangerous game and new conspiracy, the 'umma and the true Nasirites have to return the arrows of the marksmen, and uncover the game of the cheaters and swindlers.

Editor's Note: 1) Also known as the Liberation Party (Ḥizb al-taḥrīr), founded by cArif al-Nabhānī of Jordan; extremely conservative program for purification of Islam.

RESURRECTION AND REBIRTH:

THE OCTOBER WAR AND THE NEW ARAB MAN

by JOHN J. DONOHUE, S.J.

> One must rise up again ... yes, even those of us who died.
> -Adib Nahawi, "Palestinian Wedding".

> Today, on October 6, 1973 ... I was born under the patrol boats and pontoon bridges ... I came forth from the teeth of Syrian caterpillar tracks ... on the heights of Golan.
> -Nizar Qabbani, "My Face and my Passport".

June 1967 was a dark, traumatic month. It was not exactly a death, but its most visible signs of life were vocal self-criticism and somewhat negative cultural reflection. October 1973 changed all that. A new tone marked all the writings that appeared shortly after the war began; and the new tone continued to mark several short pieces in practically all the Arab dailies and weeklies long after the cease-fire. October was the birth of the new Arab man!

The theme of "the new Arab man" was not the creation of October 1973. It has been a fairly constant expression of the desire to create an Arab society viable for the 20th century. For example, an Egyptian high school text explains that the building of the new state "cannot succeed without the building of the new man". But, the creation of the new man, according to the text, is a difficult task demanding years of serious work. The "miracle" of October was that the new man showed signs of life long before the predicted term.[1]

To juxtapose June 1967 and October 1973, to put frustration and long term hopes flush against unexpected fulfillment, is to wrench developments out of their natural process. And yet, the contrast cannot be avoided. Things happened that way.

The Egyptian text sets down the qualities that must mark the new Arab man: ability to use science and technology, love of country (its land and its people, its past, present and future), self-confidence without arrogance, readiness to assume responsibility, faith in God, respect for work, etc. October, by contrast with June, was an object lesson for incorporation into a revised text: scientific preparation, ability to use modern weapons, self-confidence and faith, sacrifice for country, etc.

The feelings and reflections produced by events found rather ample expression in the Arab press. First there were the important speeches of Presidents Sadat and al-Asad, [2] and then an untold number of short pieces and poems by journalists, poets and literateurs from Morocco to Iraq. al-Ādāb, the Beirut literary monthly, published a broad sample of these writings in its Nov.-Dec. issue. [3] Reading the articles leaves one convinced that the feeling of elation engendered by October is genuine and widespread.

Certainly, it is too early to proffer judgements on the validity of this elation. The Arab authors frequently emphasize the fact that October is only the first step. However, it does seem worthwhile to offer here a selective survey of this war literature. Such a survey singles out the preoccupations of a people anxious to catch up and take part in the world of the 20th century, and may offer a sort of introduction to what will undoubtedly be a new period of Arabic literature.

The Speeches of Presidents Sadat and al-Asad

The speech given by al-Asad on October 15, and that by Sadat on October 16 do not fit the same genre as the rest of the literature surveyed. The two Presidents were speaking to their people and to the world; they were not writing for an Arab daily or weekly. The situation, politically and militarily, imposed demands and restraints. They could not voice the feeling expressed by many an author, that "no matter what happens now, things will never be the same". And yet, the themes which the two presidents expressed are, for the most part, found in the other literature.

These themes can be broadly classified under two headings 1) the Arab self-image and the Arab ability to take part in the modern age, and 2) the Arab image before the world and the Arab desire to participate in the world scene. They do not speak of the new Arab man explicitly, but the qualities they single out are those of the new man.

Classifying the themes according to "image" may seem to be the imposition of an alien structure -- but, in fact, the main thrust of both speeches is largely in psychological terms.

For Sadat the key problem of the Arab people was the gap between desire and will, between hope and reality. He chose the moment of challenge to raise the Arab will to the level of desire, to cross from despair to hope, to cure the conscience of the umma and to mend its rents. He had been confident all along that no psychological warfare could touch the basic faith of this people.

Though al-Asad states the problem as one of injured dignity, of the appearance of being easy prey, and of the pressure of the enemy to impose its will, still, at base the problem is one of will -- "the first step in this war of liberation was the complete liberation of the Arab will", liberation from the "pressure of enemy psychological warfare".

The psychological change, however, is based on the harsh realities of war. For both Sadat and al-Asad the challenge produced awakening, discovery of capacities, and self-confidence. The armed forces have shown devotion to duty, sacrifice, courage and daring, as well as a complete grasp of the age in their training, in their knowledge and in their capacity to use modern weapons.

The war for both leaders is historic in several senses. It will be recorded as a model for study, especially the Egyptian smashing of the Bar Lev Line. The defiance of Damascus and the Syrian cities is also historic. But in a very special sense, the war proves the continuity of the glorious aspects of Arab history. Sadat was confident in the outcome because he had faith in Egyptian history which embraces 7,000 years of civilization. He knew that great nations only discover their essence and true self in combat. Now the people, on the basis of his faith and theirs, have proven that 1967 was the exception and not the rule. The standard will be passed on to the coming generation raised high.

al-Asad is less vocal on this historic aspect. He merely refers to the defiance of "eternal" Damascus, and to the feats which have revived the traditions of the umma and of our fathers and ancestors. Israel was going counter to history. Now the coming generation will receive its right to a full life.

There is strong emphasis given to the world's image of the Arab in both speeches. This preoccupation is natural in that the Arab image has suffered for 25 years by continual comparison with the Israeli. But the moment of challenge changed all that. The illusions of the enemy and the myth of its invincibility were smashed.

The Arabs have won the sympathy and respect of the world -- though Sadat would prefer respect without sympathy rather than sympathy without respect. For al-Asad the war corrected the erroneous concepts about the Arabs which were taking firm root in the outside world -- "all now have esteem, wonder and respect for us".

This new respect is not illusory, it is grounded in reality. The ground for al-Asad is the defiance of Syria: death awaits all who try to debase us. Unless those who support Israel change, the anger of the Arab masses will explode.

But Sadat is much more conscious of a role in the arena of world politics. The Arab world has always played a strategic and cultural role in the world because it is "in the heart of the world and in the essence of its movement". The Arabs possess the world's most important economic riches. To forget this is ignorance and insult. "We, not Israel, are the map of the Middle East. The world must know that we can permit or prohibit".

Sadat also wishes to share in the peace of the world (the war was for peace) and to support the Russian-American detente. He points out how responsible he has been in restraining himself from using missiles which could strike into the depths of Israel. He has stayed within the Charter of the United Nations, he has been faithful to humanity. In fact, he is only completing the war against Facism and Nazism.

There are several other themes which could be pointed out.

Also, there are major differences in the two speeches which could be studied in much more detail. Here I have merely tried to point out the predominant and common themes which touch most pointedly on the changes which October wrought. I have passed over the theme of unity among the Arabs which is explicit in al-Asad's speech, but much more subtle in that of Sadat.

The Egyptian Literature

The main themes of Sadat and al-Asad are found in various forms among the selection of Egyptian writings: the crossing from despair to hope, self-confidence, grasp of the science and technology of the age, destruction of the Israeli myth by the force of the Arab will, the new image before the world, and an Arab mission in the world.

A brief piece of Tawfiq al-Hakim is illustrative:

> "We crossed over our defeat by crossing over to Sinai. No matter what the result of the battle may be, the important thing was the initial leap. It means that Egypt is always Egypt. The world thought that Egypt was asleep; but Egypt's spirit never sleeps. It may be calm, drowsy for a while, but it has its squalls and tempests, then it arises... our spirit, set free today by our heroic effort will shine forth tomorrow in formidable works produced by Egyptian thought in science, literature and art. The history of our new thought, expressing our new spirit will be written from now on".

The crossing was a natural metaphor for the Egyptian expression of the change :
Lutfi al-Khouli - "the crossing of the Egyptian man ... a new birth".
Yusuf Idris - "not only the army crossed, but the whole people ... the crossing was salvation".
Muhammad Amin al-Alim - "the Arab man crossed the walls of anxiety and despair".

For a few revolution also expressed the change:
Najib Mahfuz - "it was not just a battle, but a revolution... liberating the new Egypt ... a revolution of will and intellect and spirit".

Yusuf Idris - "it was not just the beginning of a war of liberation but the beginning of the Fourth Revolution of the Egyptian people" (following the Revolutions of 1882, 1919, and 1952). For Louis Awad it was a washing of the shame of defeat.

Perhaps the most interesting theme is that of Egyptian and/or Arab authenticity like "the spirit of Egypt which never sleeps" (T. Hakim) or "the faith in our history which embraces 7,000 years of civilization" (Sadat). It appears in various forms among other Egyptian writers:

> Lutfi al-Khouli - "this man, in Syria and in Egypt,... at the moment of the crossing became a new man, smelted in the struggle, purified of all the negative things... giving rebirth to all the positive things he inherited or gained ... all the miracle is found in this simple man once he found himself and knew his road. It is the human miracle

which bursts forth continually from every people who refuse defeat..."

Yusuf Idris - "the crossing uncovered the ordinary Egyptian man, his extraordinary force ... we did not know him, did not know he existed ... he changed from the Egyptian as he is to the Egyptian as he should be. But what we hear now is not really new. This people holds in its breast all the elements of heroism... the only change is that people have taken up arms to defend themselves, to face the enemy ... and to build a new Egypt, the Egypt in which we delight and in whom we believe ... the people defending itself and its glories, its heritage and its history, bring back to mind all former heroes from the days of Ahmas to Qutuz to Anwar Sadat".

Zaki Najib Mahmud - "every nation has unique moments in which the most special of its characteristics crystallize... these characteristics do not appear suddenly from nothing... they are there waiting the moment of crisis... when all lines meet in one point and uncover the hidden things deep in the soul... another characteristic which sets us apart is the fine sense by which we distinguish what is worthy of serious concern and what is not. We are a nation 6,000 years old... we carry on our shoulders four successive civilizations as we enter a fifth... Leonardo de Vinci stamped a cunning smile on his Mona Lisa and the critics persist in offering explanations which may uncover the secret of that inscrutable smile. I believe that there are hundreds of statues sculptured by ancient Egyptian artists... bearing smiles more enigmatic and unfathomable, it is the smile of experience with life and its mystery... if something is serious, Egypt's concern swells, its limbs move and it realizes miracles... today, we return to our true selves - namely, that quiet which enfolds a long history in which we fashioned culture and built a civilization - or rather civilizations which followed one after another".

Sayyid Yasin - "in the fire of battle appeared the authentic Arab personality which psychological warfare was trying to deform. The Arab personality is the authentic model of the national personality: deep-rooted, formed over the centuries ... a connected system of human values ... loves liberty ... tends to peace and tolerance, and is open to other peoples ... has deep faith in the historic mission of the Arab people to share in the progress of the world, now as in the past, without belittling others nor lording over them ... capable of creativity in every form".

This uncovering of the inner forces of the Egyptian and/or Arab man takes on an historical dimension in all the citations above; but for Lutfi al-Khouli the historical dimension is minimal, whereas for Zaki Najib Mahmud it is central. Mahmud even goes so far as to attribute it all to a divine plan: "the Egyptian and the Arab... knows that in the universe there is a management that provides that the scale be balanced... he knows that things move ultimately by God's will".

There are, however, explicit cautions against thinking that victory in one battle is the end of the war. Najib Mahfuz speaks of the necessity of preparation to transfer science from the level of study and comprehension to that of creativity and inventiveness. But the clearest caution comes from Muhammad Amin al-Alim. He warns that:

"the decisive element is not in the international situation, but in ourselves... we should not be content with expressing the essence of the Arab man struggling for noble human values... raising up what is in our glorious Arab heritage... but we must also plant new values and human treasures in our society and in the new victorious Arab man".

Syrian Selections

The Syrian writings in al-Adab are less than half the volume of Egyptian writings (18 pages as compared with 40). From this sample the general tone is very different. There is less lyricism and less preoccupation with a risen past, but there is still a notion of specificity.

Hanna Minah - "technology is the basis of the accomplishments of our age, but it is technology in the service of the age, for the benefit of its chief problems. This age, with this technological mastery, is our age as much as that of anyone else - rather it is our age more than anyone else's, because we are in its train, not against it. We defend its progress while our enemies try in vain to turn it back... history does not go back...the Arabs possess the achievements of the technology of this age and moreover they possess the petroleum energy without which scientific technology would never be reduced to practical technology... the Arabs have entered the age of technology using its achievements in a competent manner as the October war demonstrated... and before us, in Vietnam, that myth of incapacity to comprehend the technology of the age was smashed".

Afif Bahansi lists ten accomplishments of the war: 1) victory over the inflated, illusory, arrogant word and reliance on the word full of certainty, reality and logic; 2) change to rationality, science and planning after utopianism and improvisation; 3) winning back dignity and doing away with the legend of Israeli superiority by military competence and heroism - the victory was not a gift or a grant, no foreign state shared in it; 4) the all inclusive nationalist stand of all the Arab states; 5) liberation of petroleum energy from influence of companies and trusts... it is now in control of our will and pleasure; 6) the keys of the Western economy are dependent on our pipe lines... it will be compliant to the petroleum policy we draw up... but our role will never be arbitrary as was the role of the countries importing our petrol; 7) victory over America and imperialism; 8) support of African countries; 9) military victory will be studied as a model in military history; 10) the greatest victory is the confirmation of Arab contemporary existence, we belong to modern civilization; the battle made clear to us and to history that the Arab giant which awoke a half-century ago is today going forward with its face to the sun.

Ali Kana^{c}an, alone, gives a more extended expression of Arab history revivified but it is quite different from the Egyptian examples above:

"the enemy feared the appearance of the Arab fighting man, feared his bright cultural history, and feared, even more, that this history with its fighting glories and virtues of chivalry be resurrected". - He also sees Arab blood and earth as the key to miracles: "Arab blood was the light of our civilization and the maker of historic miracles in the life of our nation... and it will remain so. Since the battles of the Elephant and Dhu Qar till our day whenever the doors of life closed in the face of the Arab or whenever the roads were blocked there was always blood, unified, national blood. That is the magic key which creates the extraordinary, fashions miracles and returns life more brilliant than ever... from that blood come forth hidden springs in the depth of souls, springs of goodness and love, courage and tireless action".

The most lyrical of the Syrian writers is Nazar Qabbani. Apart from the piece cited at the beginning of this article, he also has a memorable piece on Damascus, the bride who has refused all suitors and match-makers for six years while she awaited the armed knight from Mount Hermon. She became melancholic. Doctors advised her to go to Switzerland or at least to Beirut where she could forget her love at the St. George Hotel and mingle with the crowds on Hamra Street, but she refused. Then, on October 6th the knight came. The city is festive - rockets and explosions, children picking up falling stars of David from the streets.

Qabbani's pieces, though captivating, are quite out of tone with the other Syrian selections. He lives in Beirut.

Palestinian Writings

In the selections from Palestinian writers practically all the basic themes are found except that of competence in use of modern weapons. October was birth, renewal, liberation from spiritual and psychological occupation, revolution, smashing of enemy myths, return to the current of history, and assertion of one's true place in the world.

The most attractive pieces, in a literary sense, are those of Mahmud Darwish. He uses well-chosen metaphors with restraint. Writing on the seventh day of the war he uses biblical allusions:

> "Today is the seventh day, the day on which God rested... God drops his old name and takes on a new name: it is the fatherland... God is the fatherland. We do not rest from work, but from defeat... it is a holiday from defeat... in the beginning was the defeat. In the new Book of our Genesis our blood is writing that the first day of this history was the Feast of Repentance for our enemy who never repented. We stand in their place to repent of our sins against the right of the homeland not liberated, the right of infants not born, the right of the future which never came. It is the day of our repentance, the day of their folly...
>
> On this day, the day (Oct. 12), the enemy celebrates the second feast in a week - the feast of tabernacles, the day of their first Exodus from Sinai. Today they went out from Sinai under the force of the Egyptian soldier... we go to war and we arrive at birth".

In another piece "The Arabs are coming", Mahmud Darwish addresses the world:

"Wait for us, world. Wait for us a bit, for we are coming to you. We are busy now fashioning the hands to reach to you... the bridges on which our voices will cross to you. Wait for us, world. Wait for us a bit... and do not play too much with the globe of the earth, it is trembling. Do not play too much, for in a short while we will be able to put it back in balance - if you wish. Wait for us, world... Our spirit is returning from captivity, clothed in a body of wheat and sun... it is returning."

"When did you remember, when ?" the world asks us.

"When you forgot us completely," we answer.

"Will you not make excuse ?" asks the world.

"Pardon was never offered". Our death alone was what took the form of pardon. We make excuse because we tarried in the womb, but birth is very hard these days... the midwife comes with the foetus, from within comes the midwife... from within. Now you know...

Do not believe that this is war, oh world... it is only the announcement of our presence. It is the way to reach you. Liberty has a voice that resembles the voice of war, but it differs, it differs... from the mouth of this rifle peace will be poured out on the sad land".

In response to the question of what the Palestinians are doing in the battle, he answers that the Palestinian seems lost in the picture because Palestine has been Arabacized and Arabism has been made Palestinian. The Palestinian is a wind, a spark; the camera cannot catch wind and spark.

The historical renewal is the theme of a piece by Abdal-Wahhab al-Kujali:

"For centuries the Arab umma has been preparing to renew its cultural journey and resume its lofty place in the procession of human progress. Our umma, thirsty for glory, reads the biographies of Muhammad, Umar, Ali and Khalid as visions of the future, not memoirs of the past. It sees in the genius of Mutanabbi, Abul-Ala, al-Kindi, Ibn Khaldun, Ibn Rushd, al-Khwarizmi and Ibn Sina a picture of our coming generations and pages of coming aspirations. Salah al-Din is a promise and the lesson of Qadisiyya and Hatin and Jerusalem is a pledge and a prayer. For centuries this fertile, prolific umma has been in labor, now it has reached the stage of birth. Birth is will, will for life through will for battle and for life. For centuries while our umma has been stripped of will, weak, condemned, dispersed, divided and plundered, the world imperialist forces competed with one another to assail it. The West considers our umma its bitter historical enemy and fears its unity and renaissance... when our umma began to awake at the beginning of the last century... fleets moved and armies disembarked to prevent the renaissance of the Arabs..."

In the other references to the awakening, however, the

point of reference is not the glory of the ancient past, but more recent decline.

For example:

> Rashad Abu Shawir: "The Arab citizen in Syria, Egypt and Palestine does not go to war to prove to himself that he is a man, or to prove that he is present in this world... the umma is awakening. Since the ages of decadence till the sixth day of this month, 1973, the Arab citizen was living in backwardness and subjugation, in a state of isolation from history and civilization, and now... the picture of stagnant Arab reality has begun - I say, begun - to dissolve. In the clear, cauterizing fire, the masses organized their energies with heroism, persistence and awareness. Finally, they knew what they wanted... what is happening on the two fronts is a vivid historical moment in which the Arab umma is welded together as it comes forth from the period of decadence... Our umma faces an awesome historical moment, everyone must participate according to his role... in order to make the turn which leads to a great Arab future".

For Mahmud Darwish it is a "re-entry into the march of history" and a "returning of Eastern history to the age of reason" with a new meld:

> "Fire tests the metal of the Arab man... if the battle is long then the operation of testing will be complete, the metal will be proven authentic and the fusing of the Arab man with different values and new convictions will be mature".

Lebanon

Although Lebanon was not directly engaged in the war as were Syria, Egypt and the Palestinians, the Lebanese literature reflects similar reactions.

The war was birth - "a brown Arab rebel cleaved open the womb of the earth and walked" (Laila Baalbeki), it was "a crossing from debasement to revolution" - a revolution like that of Russia (Suhail Idris), "a feast of repentence for our sin of June the 5th" (Ghada Simman), a war for peace (Ansi al-Hajj).

It may be useful to single out, here, a theme which though not peculiar to the Lebanese selection is well expressed by Suhail Idris - the role of the Arab writer in the struggle. Tawfiq al-Hakim, the Egyptian writer, asked for some manual work by which he could aid the war effort. Dr. Idris reflects:

> "Despite my great admiration for this creative writer, I must say that his words are more of an expression of kindness and courtesy rather than a serious treatment (of the subject). If we go into them we see that they belittle the fighting word. We are convinced that the fighting word, if charged by its author with truth and depth, is no less important and effective than a bullet. A writer does not have to live the conditions of the battle. By the penetration of his insight and depth of his awareness he can flesh

out the battle by word and expression in such a magnificent way that he gives the impression that he was there".

There were similar reflections given by Ghali Shukri, as well as support for Tawfiq al-Hakim's attitude (Nizar Qabbani, Louis Awad, Boland al-Haidari).

There seems to be a certain embarrassment among some writers concerning their role in the war. But for Suhail Idris there are no doubts about the role of literature:

> "The crossing will be a very rich subject for Arab poets and story writers... Arab literature will be a truthful witness to this great stage of our modern history, sharing by its creativity in forming the new Arab society which will play an outstanding role in the future of world society".

Reference to Arab history also occurs among the Lebanese writers. For Adonis, the reference is made in passing:

> Cutting all ties with U.S. "will assure the Arab consciousness of its existence, personality and role, and raise the Arabs to the level of historical vision which will enlighten their future. The Arabs will be faithful to their history: yesterday they shared in opening the windows of light which illumined the world, today they share in closing the windows of pestilence that choke the world".

But for Munah al-Solh, Arab specificity is much more explicit:

> There is no reason for surprise that "a nation which is ancient and feels deeply its authenticity and heritage and is bulging with competence and energy should rise up to confirm a simple share of its rights... a nation in whose personality is fixed an absolute faith in her nobility and complete desire to assert her personality... a nation whose every vein refuses anything less than being classified in the vanguard of the nations... and cannot accept any notion tending to make of the Arabs ordinary states".

Ghada Simman refers to Damascus as the Hanoi of the Arabs: "the bride of glory in the wedding of blood" - and makes a rather clever comparison based on Arab history:

> "In the old days the Arabs used to send their sons to the desert to learn poetry and horsemanship. Today send your sons, oh Arabs, to Syria and raise them there. In Syria is being formed a new Arab war ethics... this will be the story we will tell to history after a long absence".

Thus, even though Lebanon was not directly involved in the fighting the sense of change and renewal was felt. This was expressed cogently by Adonis:

> "Even we who do not know how to aim a rifle and are ignorant of the intoxication of battle; even we who saunter along the sidewalks our thoughts hanging around us in tatters; even we who greet this daily, living death, can now see through the eyes of Sinai the thread which joins poetry and bullet, face and sun..."

Iraq

The literature from Iraq is rather devoid of strong feeling. There are just a few scattered sentences indicating a new birth, such as that of Abdal-Rahman al-Rabi[c]i : "I don't know what state I am in now, but I know I am different than before... blood runs in my veins ... everything tastes different".

The most recurrent theme is that Iraq has made a revolutionary gesture in nationalizing U.S. oil interests in Basra.

In short, the literature reflects little sense of change. Where authors from other countries speak of new unity, several Iraqis repeat the old warning against Arab reactionaries and insist on Iraq's revolutionary character.

Saudi Arabia

The Saudi Arabian selections are also quite different from all the above. There is no new birth - just change in which God and religion have a share in restoring the Arabs to their true role.

> Hamud al-Badr : "God does not change what is in a people till they change themselves. (Quran 11:13) ... The Arabs changed themselves really, in fact they transformed themselves to the point that the world begins to feel the change and a large part of world opinion blesses and encourages the change ... the Arabs changed themselves and God changed them".

> Hasan Kutubi : "Everyone had ignored and forgotten that there are hidden realities in the Arab character, stronger than any force, more effective than any weapon. This force derives from their religion ... their authenticity ... the Arabs proved to the world their authenticity, superiority, and courage, and their adherence to excellent morals and noble human principles ... they proved they are worthy of the respect and amity of their friends and that by their religion and heavenly principles ... they are the best of nations raised up for the people (Quran 3:110) ... the war ... demonstrated the right of the Arabs and restored them to their honorable history".

> Abdallah al-Majid : "I will never find the sword of Ali b. Abi Talib or of Khalid b. al-Walid, nor the horse of Salah al-Din that I might use them in war. But I uncover the traces of that glory so that I may find for myself a form similar to its heroes".

Kuwait

For the Kuwaiti authors the war returned self-confidence, dignity, unity, world respect. But here also there is no new birth, just a return to normal:

Ahmad al-Saqqaf : "this umma can only be as it was in all ages, an umma of glory, heroism and sacrifice ... we should not forget that we are a great umma - extremely great, without exaggeration - a nation to which no other on earth can be compared".

Abdal-Razzaq al-Basir : "there is no need to go into details concerning the fact that the human and natural resources of this area are such as to make the Imperialists very afraid that this umma will turn its attention to its own business ... it is an integral umma which would be in need of practically nothing if it put to use all its resources. In addition, it has a great heritage and a deep rooted civilization which make it one of the nations that can compete with the strong nations ... this battle ... is the beginning of change in modern Arab history. Each of us has begun to feel a return of life and national pride and the restoration of our glories. The world ... has begun to look to us with respect whereas before it looked at us with contempt, because the world understands nothing but force"...

North Africa

The Algerian pieces are without lyricism. The war is a marker between two histories of the Arab umma, a crossing over from despair and decadence. Abdallah Rakibi salutes "those who die that we might have life with dignity in our Arab land, those who fight for the glory of the Arab man and his immortal, deep rooted history". Sa^{c}d Zahran sees the positive results of the war not as a new birth but as the effect of experience learned.

For the Moroccan writers the war is a war of liberation, a battle for existence and dignity, a realization that the only language the world understands is the language of bullets. Abdal-Karim Ghallab sees the glorious participation of the Arabs in the formation of past civilizations, Pharaonic, Islamic and Mediterranean, as a proof of their preparedness to share in modern civilization with all their force and potential in an atmosphere of peace and peaceful co-existence with all the countries of the world.

A series of Tunisian writers interviewed agree that the war will change the world's view of the Arab. In addition the war is: a proof that the Arabs can impose their will on events, a liberation from psychological complexes, a restoration of self confidence, and a confirmation that we are "the best of nations raised up for the people".

The one Libyan author represented, Ahmad al-Faqih, describes the war as a war of pride doing away with all the sad "June things" (Ḥazīrānāt). He addresses the October rains (pouring from clouds which are not from London, America or Siberia - they are our own):

> "rain down in torrents, wash off the dust and earth which cover my head and shoulders and the features of my face, wash away the rubble of defeat filling the quarters, streets and houses of my country. Only you can sow fertility in this land nearly dead from sterility".

CONCLUSION

The citations selected above and the brief summaries used to recapitulate pages of writing are not proposed as the only possible reading of this literature. In a sense, any selection of texts and themes introduces a sort of distortion. I have merely attempted to point out and illustrate what the October war meant to a good cross-section of Arab writers. I think there is little doubt that the elation found in these selections reflects the general feelings of Egyptians, Syrians, and many other Arabs.

The war was certainly a psychological liberation for even the most cautious and cynical. First of all, it was the first modern Arab war. According to all common estimates the venture should have been a disaster. The Arabs had been prey to the psychological warfare of Israel and their own previous failures - especially that of 1967. But when the war continued without collapse there was no doubt that there had been a change.

Does the change between the operation of October 1973 and the fumbling of June 1967 justify the proclamation of "a new Arab man" ? Or is the lyricism of much of the recent war literature just another example of emotional exaggeration, rising as high in October as it descended low in June ?

There are certainly concrete facts to support the interpretation that October 6 marks a turning point. Not that everything suddenly changed overnight. Things have been in process for several decades, and many of the positive elements in the October conflict were certainly in preparation shortly after the summer of 1967. They are symbolized in part by the "Corrective Movements" of 1970 in Syria and 1971 in Egypt. The damping of divisions based more on slogans than on reality was a prelude to the unity which October represented. Also the world energy "crisis" and increased oil revenues offered to Arab oil producing countries the opportunity and financial capacity to make their presence felt internationally. Perhaps the most important change was that careful military and political preparation was made to exploit the favorable situation so that on October 6 the Arabs could take matters into their own hands. The war was the calculated risk which could change the situation, or at least hasten and symbolize the change which was inevitable.

In a sense, Sadat was correct in describing 1967 as an exception. The process of development which has been going on for more than a quarter of a century was bound to show its effects. Perhaps this explains the trauma of 1967; the utter failure bred a complex. Inevitably, the release of October was magnified. The myths which the war shattered - a frequent theme in the literature - were myths which had a rather firm grip on the Arabs.

The question now is whether or not October will breed a new myth. The fairly frequent citations referring to past historical grandeur and an inbred quality of greatness make the question unavoidable. Myths are functional as long as they reflect and reinforce the reality at hand. The often cogent analysis of the Israeli myth which appears in the literature should temper the too facile expressions of inevitable greatness.

Undoubtedly, there is exaggeration in the literature. Sayyid Yasin (Egypt) criticized the Egyptian writers who before October were attacking the Egyptian personality for lacking all the qualities the same writers suddenly discovered were indelible historic qualities of the Egyptian in October. (Ahram 22/1/74 p. 5). Some of the writers also seem to attribute exaggerated importance to their own role in Arab society. One has attempted to demonstrate how the literature following June 1967 was the motivation for October 1973. This is not easy. However, some take the opposite tack as Abdul-Rahman al-Rabi^{c}i (Iraq) who wrote :

> "We are all out of employment now. While we were crying over June 1967, the Egyptian and Syrian soldiers went to war. We should drop our pens and go learn how to use a gun. The war shows that all our chatter was useless".

In short, the literature examined here has one clear value - it reflects the elation and optimism of the accomplishment of October. This psychological factor is surely important for development. But, for prognostication one should perhaps seek other indicators.

Notes

1. al-Tarbiya al-Qawmiyya : al-Dawla al-^{c}Asriyya (Cairo, Ministry of Education, 1973) pp. 11-13.

2. al-Ba'th (Damascus) 16/10/73 pp. 1-2 and al-Ahram (Cairo) 17/10/73 pp. 3-4.

3. There are several other newspaper articles not included in al-Adab which expressed the same themes and optimism. They are available in chronologies prepared by CEMAM.

SOCIO-CULTURAL CHRONOLOGY OF THE ARAB MIDDLE EAST

FOR JULY, 1973

by THE STAFF OF CEMAM

The chronicles in this number and in the previous one are articles which, in treating a single topic, draw together, in summary fashion, various references in the Arab press.

The chronology for July, 1973, which follows, attempts rather to provide a day-by-day flow of events and comments on a variety of socio-cultural topics. Such a presentation over a period of a month not only will provide a great deal of precise information but also will convey a sense of the vitality and diversity of the Arab world today.

A similar chronology covering the four months after the War of October 1973 (November-December, 1973 and January-February, 1974) has been compiled and is available separately.

A word of explanation is needed, perhaps, to clarify what is meant by a socio-cultural chronology.

First it is not political, nor is it economic, though, when political and economic events or pronouncements have a social goal or express a cultural stance, they are recorded.

For example, economic projects aimed directly at social amelioration (housing, literacy campaign, etc.) are of interest . The speech of a political leader which expresses, at least in part, a social concern or a cultural stand is also of interest. Likewise, statements by ideological groups are recorded on the grounds that ideology represents a search for a new cultural identity. In these areas the lines are not always clear; some items in the chronology may be disputable.

For the rest, the categories are fairly neat:

Arabization;	youth;	family and marriage;
humanities;	education;	ethics, mores, morality;
religion;	women;	socio-economics: syndicates,
minorities;	law;	poverty, development.

The education and socio-economic sections for Lebanon

are rather large in comparison with other countries. This stems from the very different nature of the Lebanese system. Does it show something about the processes of Lebanese society?

For North Africa the items reflect only what the Middle Eastern papers and weeklies have singled out for notice. There is no attempt to follow North Africa through the North African press.

In short, the chronology attempts to show the events, activities and thinking of Middle Eastern society as reflected in the press, thus offering one possible approach to understanding these societies in process.

TABLE OF CONTENTS

SOCIO-CULTURAL CHRONOLOGY OF THE MIDDLE EAST

FOR JULY, 1973

I. GENERAL

JULY
1973

5 -At the ILO convention in Geneva an Arab-sponsored resolution failed to obtain the required majority. As a result Arab and African labor organizations will boycott the ILO. The resolution condemned Israel for racism, and called on the ILO to send a commission to Israel to investigate charges of discrimination against Arab workmen. (AH 5/7 p.4)

10 -A film on the life of Muhammad will be financed by Libya, Morocco, Kuwait, and Bahrain. The scenario and filming will be checked by al-Azhar. The ^{c}Ulemā' of 4 countries have given their approval. Neither the prophet nor the persons of his house will be seen in the film. (HAY p.6; NAH 18/7 p.7; SAFA 23/7 p.11) Nadīm el-Jizr (Mufti of Tripoli, Lebanon) is opposed to producing such a film. (O-J 16/7 p.4)

15 -The General Islamic Congress (Amman), in a letter on the plight of Muslims in Bulgaria, says they are: 1) forced to change to non-Muslim names; 2) excluded from government jobs; 3) impoverished as long as they hold fast to their beliefs. This is attempt at genocide against the Muslim community. Arab nations having cordial relations with Bulgaria should try to save their Muslim brothers there. (SHIH p.2)

15 -Izvestia denies that USSR had anything to do with booklets against Islam and the Quran says the pamphlets were falsely attributed to official Russian publishing houses. (N p. 3; YOM 17/7 p.6)

28 -The Council of Ministers of the Federation of Arab Republics (Egypt, Syria, Libya) is studying the unification, for the three member states, of labor union legislation, social security systems, preventive medicine, and nationality. (AH p.6)

29 -Opening of World Youth Congress in Berlin, Yasir Arafat a guest of honor. One day set aside for solidarity with the Arab people. (N p.1; see also 31/7 p.1; 1/8 p.1) Arabic one of the six official languages. (N 18/7 p.1)

31 -Meeting of the Federation of Arab Workers in Construction and Building Materials Industry to be held next month in Damascus. On agenda: Condition of workers in occupied Palestine, the construction crisis in Lebanon. (AH p.4)

IIA. LEBANON: POLITICAL CRISIS; CONFESSIONAL REACTIONS

(Background: As a result of the Army-Palestinian Resistance confrontation the PM Amīn al-Hafez submitted his resignation on 15/6. On 22/6 Takieddin Solh was designated to form the new government; by July 1 he had not yet chosen his cabinet. The Syrian-Lebanese border was still closed. Muslim leaders and movements were pressing the question of their representation in "participation" (i.e., the fair distribution of governmental positions on the basis of confessional representation). The Left led by Jumblatt was demanding the Ministry of Interior (which the Right opposed).

JULY
1973

1 -Hassan Khālid (Mufti of Lebanon) rallied around him Takieddin Solh (PM designate) along with A. Yafi, K. Jumblatt and R. Karāme, to relieve the crisis. C. Chamoun, however, hardened his position. (N p.2; OJ p.3) For positions taken against Jumblatt and his insistence on democratic liberties, see MUH pp.2-3; also MUH 2/7 p.12.

3 -In a new declaration the P.S.P. and the F.N.S. set out their demands (including the Ministry of Interior for one of their members). (N p.1)

-The PM selected a 20-member Cabinet with Bahij Takieddin (of F.N.S.) as Minister of Interior, but the decrees setting up the new government were not published. (OJ p.12)

4 -The Cabinet is acceptable to the Left but not to the N.L.P. and the Kataeb. (OJ pp.1-2) P. Gemayel says the Left represents only 5% of the Lebanese. (HAY p.2; also YOM 5/7 p.2; and YOM 6/7 pp. 1,8) Jumblatt addresses meeting of parties and national and progressive forces in the Beirut Cinema. (OJ p. 12; YOM p.1; further comments of Jumblatt in N 5/7 p.1 and SAFA 5/7 p.12)

-Abdul-Latif Zein (deputy of Marjayoun), supported by Joe Hammoud (deputy of Tyr), calls for greater representation for the Shiite community and is attacked by Hamid Dakroub (deputy of Nabatieh, a partisan of Kāmel al-As'ad). (OJ p.3) The PM promises to consider the Shiite claims. (HAY p.2; for a later statement by J. Hammoud, see OJ 24/7 p.3)

6 -A communique of the Muslim associations: 1) opposes the exploitation of the Muslim movement for political purposes; 2) says that "participation" is not a confessional problem but concerns the giving of justice to the less favored classes; 3) favors the reopening of the frontier with Syria. (SAFA p.3; YOM p.2; HAY p.3)

-Musa Sadr (Shiite Imam) is thinking of resigning. His declaration follows the election of Sheikh Ali Mansur as Mufti of the Jaafarites (a new community of Shiites and Alawites of Tripoli); the election was protested by the movement of young Alawites of Ali ᶜEid. (YOM p.1; OJ p.1; cf. NAH 5/7 p.12, 6/7 p.3 and 7/7 p.3; HAY 7/6 p.3 and 7/7 pp. 1,3)

7 -The Kurdish Democratic Party of Lebanon calls for preparations for the first national congress. (HAY p.10)

8 -The Imam Musa Sadr received a delegation of Syrian Alawite Sheikhs to thank him for efforts to unite Muslim sects. (HAY p.2).

9 -After 88 days of crisis and 18 days after his appointment as PM, Takieddin Solh set up Cabinet of 22 ministers. (OJ pp. 1,12; HAY p.1; cf. reactions of MUH 8/7 and AH 9/7 p.1)

10 -Visit to Beirut of Mr. Kirilenko (N°2 in Soviet Communist Party), to award medal to Nicolas Chaoui (sec. general of the Communist Party in Lebanon). (N p.1) For political significance of visit, see OJ 8/7 pp. 1,12. Kirilenko visits Frangie and PM T. Solh, K. Jumblatt (for defence of USSR by Jumblatt, see N 17/7 pp. 1,4) and Lebanese Communist leaders. (NAH 11/7 p.1; YOM 11/7 p.2; also YOM 12/7 p.3; Dust 16/7 p.50). Karim Mroue (of P.C.L.) says the aim of the visit was the Palestine problem (YOM 16/7 p.6) but not the setting up of a Palestinian state. (N 17/7 p.1)

-Muharrir editor Tawfiq Khattab (and Sha'ab editor Mr. M. Amin Doughani) arrested for insulting President Frangie. Lively reaction to arrests. (On Khattab, see for 10/7 OJ p.2; YOM p.3; N p.3; HAY p.3; MUH p. 1,12. On Doughani, see for 11/7 N pp.1,2; YOM pp. 1,3; HAY p.3; OJ p.2; for 12/7 HAY p.3; N pp.1-2. On both, see 12/7 HAY p.3; YOM pp. 1,3: SAFA p.2). On 13/7 the two editors are released on bail. (SAFA p.2; YOM p.3; AN p.1; N p.1; MUH p.3)

11 -Complaints from the Shiites of the South that the Sunnites and Maronites received the best ministries in the new government; (NAH p.2) and from ex-PM Amin al-Hafiz that Tripoli Sunnites received none. (YOM p.12; see also HAY p.2; MUH 17/7 p.2).

12 -Reactions to representation of communities in the new Cabinet; praise from Abdul-Majid Rāfai (deputy from Tripoli, Iraqi Ba'th) (YOM p.3), and blame from ex-Pres. Chamoun (HAY p.1); Jumblatt says the confessional system prevents fair representation of the people. (N p.2; SAFA p.1; YOM pp. 1,7; MUH p.1; NAH p.3)

13 -Maronite League warns of massive (50%) presence of strangers in Lebanon. (OJ p.3; YOM p.1; NAH p.3; SAFA p.3). The Islamic associations approve the formation of the new government. (NAH p.3; SAFA p.3; for Jumblatt and the F.N.S. on the new government, see AN pp.1,3)

14 -Christian reactions to new government: Chamoun and R. Edde consider Maronites under represented (NAH p.2), P. Gemayel favors reforms of the electoral law. (YOM p.3)

-Hassan Sa'ab (president of the committee of Lebanese parties) favors changes in electoral law (N 15/7 p.2), as does Hassan Rifai (Minister of Planning). (OJ 18/7 pp. 1,2). K. Jumblatt calls for new national pact. (N p.1; YOM pp. 1,3)

17 -Jumblatt sees an Arab federation as the only solution to the Palestinian crisis. (N pp. 1,4). Georges Saade (Minister of State, Kataeb) believes that the Lebanese-Palestinian crisis calls for all Arab countries to assume their respon-

sibilities and for unity in Lebanon. (OJ 19/7 pp. 1,3). Shafiq al-Hout (Resistance spokesman) says the Resistance cannot be Lebanized since it is a revolutionary movement. (OJ 20/7 pp. 1,6; on Army-Resistance confict in the South, see AH 20/7 p.1)

21 -Islamic Association urges a march on Damascus if the Syrian border is not opened in a week. (OJ p.3)

23 -At a meeting of the Union of forces of the working peoples (Nasserist right) on the anniversary of the 1952 Egyptian revolution, Kamal Chatila attacked Col. Qadhdhafi. (OJ p.3)

24 -At another celebration of 1952 Egyptian revolution, Jumblat praises Russia; Shafiq al-Hout recalls friends of Nasser in prison in Egypt; Ibrahim Qoleilat attacks the "rectifying movement of May 15" of Sadat; Iraq is criticized. (MUH p.3; N p.1; NAH 25/7 p.2)

25 -500 people at Bourj Brajneh voice support of Qadhdhafi. al-Nahar reports Qadhdhafi's criticism of the Lebanese press for not supporting his march on Cairo. Libyan financial control of some Lebanese newspapers discussed. (NAH pp.2,3)

-Jumblatt, in discussing Sadat's 23/7 speech, urges a federation of countries bordering Israel, full liberty in all Arab countries, laicization of Arab states. (N p.1)

29 -The Shiite community speaks about its rights in "participation". (SAFA p.3; NAH p.2; MUH p.2)

30 -Speaking at meeting of Democratic Socialist Party, Kāmel al-As'ad condemns the "confessional ideology", calls for social justice and development of South Lebanon, stresses Lebanese-Palestinian relations. (MUH pp. 1,3; OJ p.3). al-Balagh presents al-As'ad as striving to form a Shiite party against the Ba'thists and Communists in the south. (6/8 pp. 4,7)

IIB. LEBANON: EDUCATION

JULY
1973

1 -At LU Fac. Ed. (Faculty of Education), meeting of 309 gvt. teachers fired last Feb. Vigilance Com. reports that prospects of rehiring are good. (OJ p.4)

4 -AUB students boycott classes, want 8 days preparation before exams. (N p.1; YOM p.5)

-Students interviewed about future status of LU Fac. Ed. tend to support Fac. (HAY p.7)

5 -Since Mon 7/6 meetings of AUB BT (Board of Trustees) on financial, academic and administrative problems. Successor rumored to Pres. Kirkwood: Dr. Samuel P. Asper. (OJ p.2) Rumor denied next day.

6 -Evening of 4, joint meeting of AUB BT and Student Council. Negative results. S. Council opposes: increase in tuition, suppression of some departments and establishment of entrance exams. BT recalls limitations from devaluation of dollar and weakness of endowment.

Boycott of exams at LU, ISS. (Institute of Social Studies) Reason: attempted selection of students by exams (questions vague, different in Arabic or French), leakage of subject questions in favor of students "belonging to one political faction". (N p.2; see also N 7/7 p.1 and OJ p.2)

7 -Joseph Choueri elected Pres. of Steering Com. of new League of Lebanese Students at AUB. Underlines importance of establishing relations with LU; makes following claims (among others): creation of business schools, problem of employment for graduates, creation of national culture. (MUH p.3)

-Five students of LU Fac. Letters (Faculty of Letters) describe their problems: no relation between curriculum and social reality, opposition by ruling class to all completely free expression of ideas, heavy program makes impossible serious preparation for exams. (MUH p.3)

8 -At completion of AUB BT (HAY p.4, MUH p.3), Chairman Howard Page gave press conference: AUB is best university of region, must pay price of such teaching. Should Lebanese gvt. intervene in management, American aid ceases immediately. (OJ p.2; NAH p.6)

-Mme Qaddura (Dean, LU Fac. Letters) cites need of building accomodating 4,000 students and costing 7 million L.L. (HAY p.4)

9 -With Libyan funds, secondary school inaugurated in Khiyyām (village, S. Lebanon). (YOM p.3; MUH 10/7 p.4)

10 -Clarification by AUB Info. Office of Page's remarks. (NAH p.6; OJ p.12)

11 -LU Rector "deplores" Page's attitude, esp. toward level of LU; says there is nevertheless a challenge there which the gvt. ought to help LU to take up. (N p.2; OJ p.2)

12 -Press Conf. of Anwar Fatayiri (Pres. NFLUS) on Page's statement. Believes Page violated all rules of hospitality, is astonished at gvt. silence, and accuses AUB of "reinforcing an attitude hostile to democratization of teaching and authentic Lebanization of ed. and culture". (N p. 3; NAH p. 6; OJ p. 2)

-PM Solh receives delegation of dismissed teachers who await their reinstatement. (HAY p.2; N p.1. See also HAY 11/7 p.6; MUH 13/7 p.5 and AN 13/7 p.2)

13 -Press Conf. of Muh. Matar (of Student Council, AUB) on Page's statement. Brings up Page's lack of propriety, recalls that all AUB students "consider LU as only national university, and protests increases in tuition. Voices student demands: next Pres. be Lebanese, system of participation be introduced, new dean for student

affairs be named. (OJ p.2; N p.1; MUH p.5; NAH p.6. See also OJ SAMEDI 21-22/7 pp.4-5)

14 -Boycott of exams at LU FacEd protesting "various selective measures" (case of sick student who was dropped). (N p.1; OJ p.2)

17 -Elections for Lebanese League of Students (rightist) at AUB. Two lists presented: one, militants of NLP (Natl Liberal Party), Kataeb and National Bloc; the other "independents". (OJ p.2)

19 -New conflict at LU FacEd: students wish to participate in deliberations before publication of exam results. (N p.4; OJ p.2)

-In revising ministerial declaration there is talk of reinstating dismissed teachers; Kataeb and Liberals are opposed. (N p.2; NAH p.6)

20 -Meeting of dismissed teachers who report on approaches made towards new gvt. (N p.1)

-Stalemate between students and profs. of Fac. of Ed., LU. NFLUS attacks Council of Faculty. (N p.1; OJ p.2)

21 -Students of Institute of Journalism,LU, boycott exam on text of Said ᶜAql as being injurious to Arabs and Palestinians. (SAFA p.12)

-Meeting of LU Council: students of 1st and 2nd years of LU FacEd will be directed to the Fac. of Letters and Science, but will keep the specialized courses of the FacEd. Council did not touch problem of deliberations of FacEd. (OJ p.2)

24 -Stalement and continued lack of deliberations for exams of LU FacEd. (OJ p.2; N p.1; SAFA p.2)

-At BAU (Beirut Arab U.) 25,000 students (5,000 of them Lebanese) pass their exams. (SAFA p.2)

25 -Students of LU FacEd prevent profs. from occupying offices, recalling that Council of Fac. has not decided on participation of students in deliberation of exam results. LU Council recalls also the principle of independence of examination Jury in relation to Council of Fac. It is, then, Dean who must make decision in present conflict. (N p.1; OJ p.12)

-70 dismissed teachers visit PM Solh; he promises whatever possible to resolve impasse. They had first met R. Rizk (Min. of Ed., Kataeb) who judged that matter depends on Council of State. (N p.1; OJ p.3)

26 -Solution found to conflict in LU FacEd.; student representatives will assist at 1st and 3rd phase of deliberations. (NAH p.6)

-During meeting at ISS, students attacked Dean Caesar Nasr as unwilling to put participation in practice.

-Dismissed teachers demonstrate before Parliament.
When Police assault teachers, Min. of Interior intervenes

and protests action. (N p.1; OJ p.3; MUH p.4; cf. MUH 27/7 p.5)

27 -New demonstrations of dismissed teachers before Parliament; new contest with police; new intervention of Min. of Interior who punishes a police officer. (NAH p.6; N p.1)

On this problem, Mr. Salām (former PM), having observed on 25/7 in Chamber that lists of dismissed teachers had been "arranged" by certain "police services of the state", Mr. Ali al-Khalīl (Min. of State) declared that dismissals were "morally void". (OJ p.2) Mr. Moukheiber (also Min. of State and Min. of Ed. at time of dismissals) maintained that Council of State alone is able to decide matter. (N 29/7 p.2)

29 -Press Conf. of Anwar Fatayiri (Pres., NFLUS). He reveals "plot" which aims to set a part of professors against students, asks why LU budget for coming year has not yet been promulgated, states that gvt. delays installation of certain Lebanese teachers to keep foreign teachers. States usual demands: construction of Fac. of Letters and Ed. at Shweifāt, creation of technical Faculties, real application of law to full-time profs., reinstatement of dismissed teachers. (OJ p.2; NAH p.6; N p.1)

31 -In series of interviews, BAU students explain why they choose this university (the problem of language, etc.). (MUH p. 3)

IIC. LEBANON: SOCIAL AND ECONOMIC PROBLEMS

JULY
1973

1 -Social unrest. Lawyers in Zahle have been on strike since 27/6 to force the authorities to fill a number of vacant posts. (OJ p.2) Beirut Lawyers express support. (3/7 OJ p.12; HAY p.3) The Minister of Justice promises to fill the vacant posts before the end of August . (13/7 OJ p.2)

-Taxi drivers cut the Zahle-Baalbek road to protest against unlicensed taxis. (N p.2)

-Master-artisans of South Lebanon ask for an extension of social security benefits to themselves. (OJ p.4)

2 -al-Safa carried an account of the association of Women of Jabal Amil founded 3 years ago; its 400 members sponsor social centers for girls, 2 dispensaries, 2 schools for medical assistants. (2/7 p.2)

3 -The Union of Arab Bakery owners, going beyond the authorization of the Ministry of Economics, decided to increase the price of bread by 5 piasters. (1/7 N p.1; OJ p.2) The Ministry decides to prosecute these violators. A rival union advises bakers to await the formation of the new government. (3/7 OJ p.2; N p.4; HAY p.4; see also 10/7 HAY p.4; YOM p.3). Various protests against the high price

of bread. (4/7 YOM p.4; 5/7 N p.1; 6/7 SAFA p.2; YOM p.3; N p.1) Bakers defend themselves. (4/7 YOM p.3; HAY p.4) Workers unions protest the high price of bread and urge the authorities to close shops of violators. (9/7 YOM p.3) Bakers meet with the Minister of Economics and agree to improve the quality of the bread. (18/7 YOM p.3)

5 -A meeting called to prepare for the 7th National Congress on Development (to be held Nov. 24-25). The theme: "Strategy for the Arab Scientific and Technological Revolution: Creation of the atmosphere for scientific and technological progress". (YOM p.3 See also YOM 26/6 p.3 and NAH 26/6 p.6)

-Charles Helou (ex-President), attending a meeting in Canada of French-speaking parliamentarians, discusses Lebanese bilingualism and culture. (YOM p.3)

8 -Syrian frontier closure has brought about a social crisis: paralysis of various sectors, unemployment, etc. Elias al-Habre (National Federation president; member of the Communist party) announced a demonstration for Friday 13/7. (OJ p.2; HAY p.3; YOM 9/7 p.2) Demonstration cancelled because of the formation of the new government, but the Federation issued a call for: the suppression of article 50 of the Work Code (arbitrary dismissal); a struggle against high prices; and a just rent law. (10/7 N p.1; OJ p.2)

12 -Growers and exporters of fruit ask for the suppression of the Fruit Office and the use of its budget to aid exportation and the construction of packaging factories. The closure of the Syrian border holds up 30,000 tons of fruits. (HAY p.4; OJ 19/7 p.10)

-Following the government's authorization of importation of Egyptian watermelons, planters from the South demonstrate in front of the Parliament, 5 are arrested. (HAY p.4; YOM p.4; N p.2)

-New tension between the tobacco growers and the Tobacco Administration; the latter was planning to destroy the excess crops grown in areas planted without permission. (HAY p.4)

17 -Meeting of the committee of the GWF : 1) invites the PM to take account of the union demands in his ministerial statement and 2) forms a committee to follow the problems of rents, high prices, arbitrary lay-offs.

18 -The National Federation asks the Minister of Work and of Social Affairs not to give any more permits to new unions, since the multiplicity of unions only weakens the worker movement. (YOM p.2; N p.1)

-Meeting of the economic organizations about the closing of the Syrian border; commercial, banking and industrial leaders blame Syria which, they say, "treats Israel better than Lebanon". (For different reports see SAFA p.2 and OJ p.10)

19 -Meeting today in Beirut of Arab chambers of commerce. OJ publishes the points of a Lebanese note against Syria. (OJ p.3; NAH p.2)

-Beirut firemen, unable to get a hearing with the Beirut municipality, met to find ways to force the government to give them a definite status, like that of the military or of civil service. (YOM p.4)

20 -Arab chambers of Commerce, Industry and Agriculture meet about the closing of the Syrian border. (OJ p. 10; SAFA p.2)

21 -Demonstration of fruit growers of Tyre and Sidon demanding government support. (N p.1; SAFA p.2; OJ p.10)

25 -People of Badāwī (on the coast road north of Tripoli) block the road in protest against the number of accidents and lack of government control of traffic. (MUH p.12; N p.1; cf. MUH 29/7 p.4)

27 -At Qana, near Tyre, 500 persons block the road protesting 15 day's lack of water.(N p.1). Similar demonstrations in the South, in the Beqaa, in Koura (north Lebanon). (Cf. N 28/7 p.1; 29/7 p.4; 4/8p.1; see also MUH 29/7 p.4; YOM 3/8 p.5)

-250 workers on strike at light metal plant at Haret-Hreik because of salary, working conditions. On 28/7 strike ends, strikers win gains. (N p.1; cf. 28/7, 29/7 and 31/7 p.1; OJ 28/7 p.3 and 29/7 p.2)

IIIA. EGYPT: RELATIONS WITH LIBYA

(Background: Qadhdhafi had been in Egypt since 22/6. At first he held political conversations on union with Sadat; then he met Egyptian journalists and writers especially on June 30.)

JULY
1973

Qadhdhafi's Visit to Egypt

1 -Meeting 1/7 with some journalists, Qadhdhafi accused S. Arabia of being reactionary and of causing harm under the guise of religion. (YOM 2/7 p.1) Reaction of Egyptian journalists: Egypt began the revolution 20 years ago and has no need of advice (Musa Sabri, editor of Akhbar al-Yom); this is not the time for spreading ideologies but for acting to recover territories; if communism and capitalism divide the world, Libya divides the Arabs by its hostility to certain regimes; Egypt does not repress marxists, they work in the government; Libya cultural revolution was imported from China. (YOM p.6)

-Sadat and Qadhdhafi hold talks with ASU parliamentary union. Qadhdhafi's "third way of the world" (neither communist nor capitalist) is: socialist for the economy, unaligned for politics, and, for philosophy, it holds to religion, Islam being the perfect example of the values of the philosophy of heavenly religions. The Libyan revolution is inspired by the Charter; the popular committees are real democracy, even if there are excesses. (AH pp. 1,4; selected texts in YOM 2/7, SAFA 2/7 p.6)

2-3-Sadat and Qadhdhafi hold talks with leaders on the ASU. 1/7 Talk of Muh. Hāfiz Ghanim (Sec.-Gen. of CC of ASU), of Sadat, and of different secretaries of the ASU. (YOM 2/7 p.1)

Some prefer a union by stages, others a federal union; others object, saying Egyptians do not know one another well enough.

Sadat recalls that they are talking but not deciding; it is for the people to decide.

Further explanations of Qadhdhafi on "Third Way": what exists in Libya is consequence of the Arab revolution. The world thinks that Islam is reactionary, but in reality it is a permanent revolution constantly renewed, a scientific revolution capable of explaining all that happens; if we fail to understand it, we are behind times, as if all innovation were atheism or apostasy. If we do not fight for liberty, we could get along with Israel; but if we fight for our nationalism, we need a creed: the third way. (AH 2/7 pp. 1,4; YOM 3/7 p.6; MUH 3/7 p.8)

6 -Qadhdhafi explains his ideas on union to the Council of Ministers.

-With Sadat, Qadhdhafi meets women's groups of the ASU: Sadat: the woman is the basis of the family, she preserves our values and has a great role in the struggle. "We are obliged -- because we are wegded in by all the blocs -- to fall back on our own resources, on those things that make up our heritage, and all this is tied to our beliefs, so as to maintain our identity, our solidity and our resistance". (AH 6/7 pp.1, 7; YOM 7/7 p.3; MUH 7/7 p.8)

Qadhdhafi: In the West and in the communist world, the woman has abandoned her nature, she has become a man, the family is corrupted and destroyed; the ideal family gives to the woman the rights which accord with her nature; this is what Islam does. Libya does not yet completely apply the Sharia because that needs education. (AH pp.1,7; YOM 7/7 p.3)

-Before Qadhdhafi's departure Muh. Hasanayn Haykal expressed scepticism about the union: differences of ideology and customs, the cultural revolution vs. the sovereignty of the law... (AH p. 3)

-Egypt keeps its distance: bad treatment of Egyptians in Libya, the Islamic law in place of modern development, fear of being dragged into a conflict because of the imprudence of Qadhdhafi. (SAFA p.6)

9 -Cairo proposes gradual Egypt-Libya union; thus no fear for Libyans for their wealth nor for Egyptians, regarding cultural revolution. (HAY p.8)

-Musa Sabri, Akhbar al-Yom (Cairo), opposes Egypt-Libya merger as long as Libya's goals differ from Egypt's. -The "cultural revolution" in Libya should be subjected to laws binding both the governed and the governing. Egypt insists on sovereignty of the law. -As for Libya's desire to bring legislation under Islamic sharia, this could be left to the individual governorates (muḥafaẓat) in the combined state ; as in the United States, each state has its own legislation. -Qadhdhafi's "Third Outlook on the World" is already contained, in principle, in the Charter. -Important divergences exist between the foreign policies of the two nations, especially regarding the USSR. (YOM p.6; SAFA p.6)

-Unsigned letter from Cairo in al-Balagh on the two present orientations in Nasserism, al-Qadhdhafi's and Egypt's: Qadhdhafi's "Third Outlook"; Egypt's refusal to consider itself a "religious state"; the presence of 6 million Copts makes Egypt cautious about the "Third Outlook"; Egypt has already made much progress, no need for further elucidation of Nasserism; states built on religion are isolated from modern age. (pp.4-6)

-The same weekly, on Nasserite left vs. al-Qadhdhafi, cites (from Roz al-Yusuf discussion) the words of A-Sittar Tawīla and Ahmad Abbas Sālih; explains Nasser's approval of Marxism. (p.6-7)

The Libyan Unity March

19 -Thousands of Libyans, "marching" in cars and buses towards Egyptian border, carry petition for President Sadat in Cairo. Petition, written in blood, calls for immediate Egypt-Libya

merger. March began yesterday morning at Ras Jadir, near the Tunisian border, is planned to go about 2500 kilometers. (YOM p.1; N p.4; SAFA pp.1,12; NAH p.1)

-Pres. Sadat urging prudence on Col. al-Qadhdhafi in pushing the merger. Egypt wants unity, but only after serious consultation, not before. "Unity March" provides opportunities for enemies of unity and of the Revolution. (AH pp. 1,6; YOM p.1; N p.4; SAFA pp. 1,12; NAH p.1)

-Mr. Muh. Hāfiz Ghānim (First Secretary of Central Committee of the ASU) in Damascus for talks with Ba'th party, interrupted talks to fly to Libya, to discuss "Unity March" with Libyan leaders. He reportedly told them that, due to present circumstances, Egypt will not allow any demonstration or "sit-in", peaceable or otherwise. (AH pp. 1,6; YOM pp. 1,6; N p.4; SAFA pp.1,12)

-The ASU authorities send welcome to Libyan brethren, proposed to send delegations of Egypt's "constitutional and political institutions" to meet them at the town of Marsah Matruh, inside Egyptian border. ASU frowns on idea of "sit-in", suggests that the Libyans choose 100 marchers to complete the trip from Marsah Matruh to Cairo. (AH pp. 1,6; YOM p.1; NAH p.1).

NOTE: reference to Egyptian "constitutional and political institutions" recalls a point made during al-Qadhdhafi's discussions with ASU, which feels that the methods of Libyan "people's Revolution" are not compatible with Egypt's preference for achieving change within the framework of political and constitutional institutions.

-Front-page editorial of al-Yom is entitled "A march which has no justification".

20 -Popular encounter, between the Libyan Unity Marchers and delegations of Egyptian ASU, begins today at Marsah Matruh, will last two days. (AH p.1) About 50,000 Libyan marchers. (SAFA p.12)

-al-Nida remarks: enthusiasm of al-Qadhdhafi knows no bounds, but Sadat opposes all demonstrations. (p.1)

-While Egyptian ASU is asking marchers to halt at Marsah Matruh and send delegation of 100 to go on to Cairo, Libyan radio is encouraging the marchers not to halt. (N p.1)

-Cairo radio says that at their last meeting, Sadat and al-Qadhdhafi agreed to carry out merger through two popular referenda, one in 1973, other in 1974. (N p.1)

-National Conscientization Movement (Beirut Sunni political grouping) sent message to al-Qadhdhafi to halt marchers at Marsah Matruh. (N p.2)

21 -Unity Marchers, penetrating beyond Marsah Matruh towards Alexandria. Egyptians stop them with barrage of 100 cars.

-Egyptian Minister of State for Youth, Dr. Kamāl Abu Majd, led delegation of 400 Egyptians to the proposed popular congress at Marsah Matruh. (N pp. 1,3)

-A Libyan bulldozer, escorted by two Libyan police cars, wrecked the customs huts, etc., at the border station of Solum. (N pp. 1,3) Note:A symbolic act: people's will demolishes barriers.

-In message Sadat urges Qadhdhafi to tell marchers to stop at Marsah Matruh, rejects argument that Libyan leadership is not responsible for march. (AH pp. 1,3; N pp. 1,3) Qadhdhafi replies: I have submitted my resignation. I myself was surprised by the announcement of the March. There is nothing to fear from the March. (NAH p.1) Qadhdhafi cables marchers to follow directives of Egyptian leadership. (AH p.1)

-It is announced that al-Qadhdhafi tendered resignation as President of Revolutionary Council on July 11. (AH p.1; SAFA pp. 1,12)

22 -Unity Marchers returned to Libya; 1200 vehicles used. (AH p.1; N p. 1; NAH p.10)

-21 leaders of march reach Cairo by plane, are met by ASU officials. (AH p.1; N p.1) Maj. Mustafa al-Khurūbī (of Libyan Revolutionary Council) is also in Cairo. (N p.1)

-Radio Libya: Revolutionary Council refuses to accept al-Qadhdhafi's resignation. (N p.1; NAH p.10)

-Sadat is ready to accept proclamation of Egypt-Libya unity on Sept.1. (NAH p.1)

25 -Committee of Libyan Unity March, in message to Sadat, congratulates him on Egyptian revolution, hopes that under his leadership revolution will continue in its three dimensions: religious, nationalist, democratic. (AH p.1)

27 -Committe, members of Parliament and of ASU, on its way to Libya to congratulate Libyans on al-Qadhdhafi's decision to remain in office. (AH p.1)

Comments on the Proposed Egypt-Libya Unity

5 -Article by Farīd al-Khatib expresses the Egyptian reservations on proposal, and discusses the Islamic aspects of unity. (SAY p. 18).

23 -Cartoon for anniversary of Egyptian revolution shows a tree labelled "July 23rd Revolution". One branch is "The September Revolution" (i.e., Libyan revolution), the other is "The Movement of Rectification" (i.e., when Sadat took power from Ali Sabri, May 1971). Deceased President Jamal A-Nasir, sitting on a nearby cloud, reads from the Quran a text describing a tree; its roots are firmly in the ground, its branches reach to the sky. (AH p.5)

-Article on "The Long Libyan March" discusses al-Qadhdhafi's motivation: he wanted to show that idea of unity is not his alone and that the cultural revolution is working, and to provoke discussion in Egypt. (BAL pp. 16-18)

24 -al-Safa editorializes that al-Qadhdhafi has played on popular sentiment against political superstructures in each state. But slogans and symbolic gestures neither create nor organize unity. (p.1)

25 -Two articles on Libyan-Egyptian relations by E. Saab in OJ. The first (25/7 pp.1,12) lists factors favoring al-Qadhdhafi's appeal to Egyptians: money, Quran, present political conjuncture. The second (26/7 pp. 1,7) speaks of Sadat's prudence; he hesitates to cut himself off from King Faysal of Saudi Arabia to go along with al-Qadhdhafi.

26 -Article on Unity March discusses al-Qadhdhafi's ideas on Islam and Egypt's fears that the experience of Syria-Egypt union may repeat itself with regard to Libya. (SAY p.20)

27 -Haykal, to the Franco-Arab Press Ass'n in Paris, says: 1) Yes, to immediate and total merger of Egypt and Libya; 2) al-Qadhdhafi got idea of cultural revolution from Haykal, after the latter's return from China; 3) Criticism of Egyptian bureaucracy, bourgeoisie, leftist intellectuals, and immobilism. (SAFA pp.1,6)

30 -Article by Riyāḍ Farḥāt: Egypt-Libyan unity will be realized only if Egypt decides to go to war. (BAL pp. 4-7)

VIIB. EGYPT: OTHER POLITICAL DEVELOPMENTS

JULY
1973

17 -Before ASU Central Committee yesterday, Pres. Sadat spoke of a new document, now in preparation, on the changing world situation, to be presented before coming National Congress (of ASU). Purpose of document is to clarify National Charter, to avoid certain tendencies to interpret Charter in a Marxist sense. ASU is to consult the people's opinions in drawing up this document, in accordance with Egypt's concern for dialogue within framework of political institutions. (AH p.1; YOM p.1)

18 -Delegations of Egyptian Professional Unions arrived in Beirut yesterday, touring Arab countries about proposed Arab People's Congress in Cairo next September. (YOM p.5). Among delegates are Dr. Mustafa al-Barada'i and Dr. Ibrahim Badawi; they met Lebanese personalities: PM. T. Solh, Rashid Karami, Kamal Jumblatt, Abdallah Yafi, and Wafiq Tibi (VP of Arab Journalists), who is representative of the committee in Lebanon. (N 19/7 p.2)

Dr. al-Barada'i (head of the Egyptian Lawyer's Union) explained: goal of Congress is to search for the free Arab man, that he may awake after having been lost by events. In many places there is no freedom of opinion, only domination. Citizens have lost confidence in their rulers, and ties to the umma and the watn are weakening. All should be made aware of Israel's aims: the long-range aim is Arab civilization. (N p.2)

NOTE :

The Arab Lawyers Federation initiated talk since May of holding a Congress of Arab Political Forces, involving parties, movements, federations and unions. The ASU was also involved. The aim of this congress would be: to strike at American interests, to utilize the oil weapon, to improve Arab information media.

-Delegation of Egyptian ASU in Damascus for discussions with Syrian Ba'th leaders on coordination between the two political organizations. Participants in the talks include Muh. Ḥāfiz Ghānim (First Secretary of the ASU Central Committee) and Abdal Haman (Assistant Sec. General of the Ba'th party). (SAFA p.6; AH 17/7 p.6) After interruption due to Mr. Ghanim's trip to Libya, talks continued; al-Ahrām for 22/7 reported that a program for joint action is being prepared.

The Anniversary of the July 23rd Revolution

23 -Three items on al-Ahrām editorial page concern the anniversary: the column "Ḥadith al-Nas" dwells on the political situation, including the Palestinian problem and proposed Egypt-Libya merger. The column "Ra'y al-Ahrām" extols Arab and Egyptian authenticity the assertion of Egyptian personality, and the achievement of Aswan Dam.

Thirdly, signed article by Dr. A-Malek 'Udah on "The Basic Values of the July 23rd Revolution": 1) Revolution changed mentality from village and rural to industrial; from regional, tribal and sectarian to mentality of the citizen. 2) Revolution also opened Egypt to impact of currents from outside. 3) Egyptian youth support the break from the old society with its injustices in order to create new revolutionary society. (AH p.5)

NOTE: Article is significant since the writer was one of those expelled from the ASU.

-Editorial in al-Muharrir (p.1) praises July 23rd Revolution. "The secret of its greatness is that it is not just another new mass of words, nor does it flood the people with mere theories and ideas, but it broke out, then grew and developed because it was a dynamic movement and did not miss any opportunity to destroy the nation's enemies within and without".

24 -Sadat's speech on anniversary of revolution dealt with Nāsir's accomplishments, Soviet-American policy towards Egypt, Egypt's inner strength, Arab Unity, Libyan Unity March. (AH p.1; MUH p.8; N p.1) (See also below, Sadat's call for popular dialogue.)

The Call For People's Dialogue

24 -In July 23rd speech, Sadat calls for "a period of thinking and planning" in which the masses will be invited to take part in free and open dialogue on the changing world situation. The outcome will be presented at September National Congress (of ASU). (AH p.1,ff.)

26 -Parliamentary Commission to prepare for dialogue has begun its meetings under the chairmanship of Dr. K. Abu Majd (Min. of State for Youth and Chairman of the ASU Youth Secretariate). (AH p.1) The Commission has divided Egypt into six sectors; officials have been nominated to direct dialogue. Four sectors are regional, but fifth covers universities, research institutes, judiciary; sixth comprises labor unions and youth organizations. At

open sessions of Parliament citizens will be invited to propose their ideas. General theme: influence of recent changes on government policy. (AH 27/7 p.1)

The New Youth Political Organization

25 -At Cairo University ceremony yesterday, Pres. Sadat announcing inauguration of new youth organization (in ASU), said: -Youth is the majority today and the power tomorrow. -Youth is the guardian of the 1952 Revolutionary thought. -Revolution is two-fold: political and social. -No political liberty without social liberty.

-Abdal-Nasir rejected dictatorship of one class (no matter which class) over others. There is to be no class dictatorship, but democracy, and the alliance of forces of working people. -This alliance gives the specific stamp to our application of socialism . You must deepen your understanding of socialism.

-Your activity must be based on science, patriotism, be derived from the authentic nature of this people, with its force and its belief. (AH pp.1,ff.; SAFA 26/7 p.6)

-Speech by Dr. Kamāl Abū Majd (Sec. of Youth for ASU and Min. of State for Youth): New organization is based on 3 principles: (1) adhesion to ideology (fikr) of July 23rd Revolution, which includes belief in God and in the Heavenly Missions, belief in liberty, Arab Socialism and Arab Unity; (2) building of new Egyptian man capable of bearing his responsibilities; (3) opening on the world, to see ourselves on the world map, and defining our capacities for serving goals of national action in our country. (AH p.7)

-Speeches by representatives of different sectors of Egyptian youth:

:Peasant youth: Revolution has made peasant lord of his earth, and has restored to the venerable Egyptian peasantry its dignity.
:Working youth: we support solidarity with all struggling and peace-loving nations; we are with Pres. Sadat in his struggle to preserve progressive thought of Revolution against world reactionary influence.
:Students: we will adhere to thought of Nāṣir, who taught that revolution is science of complete social change.

:Young womem: Socialism is unthinkable if half the population has it's hands tied, and is constrained by values and ideologies which are no longer acceptable. Revolution has given women more of her legal rights.
:Children (a representative of "Vanguard" organization which is to prepare young children to become members of ASU organizations): We are citizens who believe in our Lord and are proud of our Arabism. (AH p.6)

-Photos of inauguration rally. (p.10) One photo shows Dr. Abu Majd presenting Sadat with copy of Quran, gift from New Youth Organization. (AH p.10. For continuation of the story on the Youth Organization, see 29/7 below.)

27 -Meeting with Faculty and students of Alexandria University July 26, Sadat said: -Dialogue he asked for in July 23rd speech must include not only politics, economics etc., but also ideological steadfastness (sumūd). Need of new economic openness. -Academic

curricula must be changed to bring us into the atomic age.

-Besides political domination Israel seeks cultural domination, i.e., to keep the Arabs backward, claiming that "Israel is science, industry, technology, while we (the Arabs) remain as the world of backwardness". We, who survived Tartar and Crusader invasions, will survive Zionist invasion.

-Cases of students of Alexandria University accused of stirring up trouble will be handled by Student Union. (AH pp. 1,6)

-Reply of Dr. Lutfi Durayd (Pres. of Alexandria U.) to Pres. Sadat: -Welcomes measures bringing education into line with modern age. -The "State of Science and Faith" includes democracy, social justice, concern for morals and education, science, technology and economic development. -Our university students have good intentions, but they are in danger of being exploited by deviationists.

-On the same occasion, Mustafa Jamāl (Pres. of Student Union) presented Pres. Sadat with a "pledge of allegiance" from the students, written in their blood. He said: -The students support Sadat. -Have followed only one "orientation", namely Egypt, her land and her liberty, in a framework of patriotism and Arab nationalism. (AH p.7)

29 -"Remarks on the problems of youth", article by Rajab al-Bana, on new youth organization: -New organization should work with other agencies working with youth. -Our guidance agencies need a new spirit and a new firm consistent policy. This work has suffered from too frequent changes and shifts of policy since the early years of the Revolution.

-Guidance, while aiming at unifying all sectors of youth, should take into account the different characteristics and needs of particular sectors, e.g., working and peasant youth.
-Much research has been done on Egyptian youth. Use should be made of its results. (AH p.5)

30 -Leadership Congress of new Youth Political Organization met yesterday to discuss Sadat's speech (cf. 25/7) and decree founding the organization. Dr. Kamāl Abū Majd spoke; the organization is an educative organization for building the new Egyptian man; youth must distinguish between genuine Nasserism and those using it as cover for destructive aims. (AH pp.1,4)

VIIC. EGYPT : RELIGIOUS AFFAIRS

JULY
1973

4 -A-Halim Mahmud (Sheikh of al-Azhar), at meeting of Academy of Islamic Research, appealed to world political and intellectual leaders to stop the persecution of Muslim minorities, which is contrary to the treatment of Muslims towards minorities, to moral principles, to the laws of UN and to rights of man. (AH p.1; HAY p.8; YOM p.6; also YOM 3/4 p.6)

5 -World Congress of Muslim Ulema to be held in December 1973 at al-Azhar. Subjects: Muslim unity, oppression of Muslim minorities. (AH p.4)

6 -A. Aziz Kamil (VP of Religious Affairs and Minister of Awqaf) meets Saudi Arabian officials about sending of teachers from al-Azhar. He also receives president of Higher Council for Family Planning. (AH p.6)

8 -Islamic Research Academy to publish encyclopedia of Quran; will list terms, their simplified meanings, historical and geographical references. (AH p.4)

9 -High Committee, formed under Pres. Sadat, to plan celebrations of al-Azhar millenary; will begin officially with recital of Friday prayer at al-Azhar next 7 Ramaḍān. (AH p.4)

10 -SCIA (Supreme Council for Islamic Affairs) to provide Islamic aid to Dahomey: grants for students from Dahomey to study in Egyptian institutions, chairs of Islamic studies in Dahomey Universities, and teachers of Arabic for Dahomey schools. (AH p.4)

12 -SCIA plans the 13th Abu Bakr al-Siddīq Congress in Alexandria, to be attended by Muslim scholars and jurisprudents from 73 nations. (AH p.4)

15 -Ministry of al-Azhar Affairs announces opening of institute for al-Azhar religious education at Sūhaj. (AH p.4)

-<u>al-Shihab</u> reprints article from daily <u>Akhbar al-Yom</u> (Cairo) on "The destruction of the faith in the hearts of Muslims: this is the goal of a deliberate plan". It describes intellectual, ideological and spiritual campaign waged by "them" against Islam in Egypt: imported doctrines, debasement of al-Azhar, repression of "Islamic Movement". (SHIH p.4)

<u>NOTE:</u> The term "Islamic Movement" is frequently used by this magazine in referring to the Muslim Brethren.

17 -Speech on Christian-Muslim relations by SCIA head Tawfiq 'Uwayḍa at the Vatican in December 1970, has been translated into English, French, Spanish, Filipino, and Swahili. This was done at request of certain government officials, including Pres. Senghor of Senegal. (AH p.6)

20 -According to a statement by A-Munim Maghrabī (Pres. of High Council for Awqaf), Awqaf income is to finance housing and other projects in different governorates, also Islamic projects. Statistics on Awqáf income given. (AH p.6)

21 -Sheikh al-Azhar, speaking for Academy of Islamic Research, says every Muslim should know enough Arabic to recite the <u>shahada</u>, perform <u>dhikr</u> and, if possible, to read some of the Quran. Values of Quran are tied to the language in which it "came down". Arabic is bond of unity among Muslim peoples. An imperialist plot aims to substitute Latin for the Arabic alphabet in transliteration for certain African languages. Keeping Arabic as language of transliteration will preserve the Arab-Islamic ties of the cultures of these countries. (AH p.4)

22 -Sheikh al-Azhar congratulates Pres. Sadat on the 21st anniversary of the July 23 Revolution: God helped you in the Movement of Rectification (the elimination of the Ali Sabri group May 1971) in order to protect Islam, his true religion. He expects you to strengthen his creed and exalt his sharia in our Muslim society. (AH p.4)

25 -Board of Awqaf on the anniversary of the July 23rd Revolution announces: For building the state of Science and Faith; for supporting alliance of people's working forces; for preserving substance of the creed and of deep-rooted Arab values; for continuation of creative action leading to freedom, socialism and comprehensive Arab unity, we pledge to you (Sadat) our support. (AH p.5)

26 -Press conference of Dr. A-ᶜAziz Kāmil (Min. of Awqaf and Vice-Premier for Religious Affairs):
1) he proposes establishment of Supreme Council of Islamic Institutions and Boards, to coordinate their role in the struggle; 2) he will elevate level of mosque service, and improve preparation of Imams; 3) Islamic research should be strengthened; 4) Awqaf revenues will be used for da'wa (propagation of Islam); 5) since Revolution, number of mosques attached to Ministry rose to 4926, of which 1360 were formerly private mosques; 6) Ministry has established five centers for interest-free loans. (AH p.6)

-Mr. Tawfīq al-'Uwaydā (head of SCIA) has discussed Islamic relations with the head of the Religious Affairs Dep't of Indonesia's ruling party. Egypt will provide grants for 10 Indonesian Muslims to study at Egyptian institutions. (AH p.6)

28 -Yesterday, Pres. Sadat attended prayer at the Sayādayn Mosque, near Cairo, one of the little mosques that he is fond of frequenting. (AH p.1)

-Tomorrow, moon-watching begins for Rajab new moon in Egypt and other Islamic countries on the same latitude. Hopefully this date (1 Rajab), as well as 1 Ramadan, can be unified for all Islamic countries. Astronomical observatories in Saudi Arabia indicate Monday July 30 as probable date of 1 Rajab; observatory at Halwan, Egypt, indicates Tuesday, July 31. (AH p.6)

NOTE: for al-Ahram, at least, Halwan was correct. Some other Arab papers followed Saudi Arabian dating.

29 -Mayoralty of Cairo repairs ancient 'Umar 'Ibn al-'Ās mosque, to be ready for Friday prayers on last Friday of Ramadan, when Sadat is expected to assist. (AH p.4)

31 -Dr. A-'Azīz Kāmil announces:
:Role of the mosques to be developed; they will render social services (as shelters, for engagement ceremonies, in care of orphans) to the people, in addition to prayer services. Imams are to learn First Aid etc.
:Secretariate for Islamic Congresses to be established.
:Supervision of "Islamic centers" to be unified.
:Certain labor laws to be relaxed in favor of employees of former private mosques which are being transferred to Ministry of Awqāf.
:Egyptian religious institutions will help in education of youth in other Muslim countries.
:1000 ḥalaqāt (centers for learning to memorize Quran) are to be built. (AH p.4)

VIID. EGYPT: MISCELLANEOUS

JULY
1973

2 -Decree authorizes return to Egypt, at government expense, of ashes of emigres. (AH p.3)

3 -Executive Council of UNESCO, due to meet in Cairo on the 17th, will study two projects of the centers of research: on development of human resources, and on educational means to combat illiteracy and to preserve Arab-Muslim heritage. (AH p.4)

-Arab Economic Unity Council of Arab League meets in Cairo to study systems of commerce and transport. (AH p.6)

4 -Murad Ghalib (Minister of Information) meets Journalists Union Council, states that the press ought to conduct a democratic dialogue on problems of the public. (AH p.4)

-Agreement on cultural cooperation between Egypt and Tunisia for exchange of artists, visits of journalists, writers. (AH p.4)

6 -Nominations of members to the administrative secretary generals of the Unions and Syndicates close today. Proportion of representation of different governorates. (AH p.6)

9 -Fiftieth anniversary of women's movement in Egypt: their struggle for equality with men; their public demonstrations against imperialism; women's rights leader, Huda Sha'rāwī, is honored as the pioneer. (MUH p.10)

-Ministry of Higher Education decides to establish a "private" (i.e., tuition-paying) university, to absorb overflow of students unable to get into existing Egyptian universities. Exodus of Egyptian students to Lebanese and foreign universities, often done illegally, will be reduced.

The Council of Universities is also studying project of incorporating colleges and institutes at Minya into an independent university. (AH p.1)

-Twenty persons (mostly students) to appear in court at Alexandria beginning next Saturday (July 14) on charges of organizing a movement hostile to regime, calling for students demonstrations, etc. (AH p.1; YOM 10/7 p.6; HAY 10/7 p.8)

16 - al-Balagh publishes declaration issued by the "Nasserite journalists" during elections of Council of Press Syndicate in Egypt. Slate supported by the dismissed writers won. Declaration, dated May 18, 1973, and signed "The Expelled Nationalist Journalists", states that the problems have arisen due to a group of royalist journalists at work in all papers. They used May 15 Movement of Rectification as excuse to expel nationalists, are more dangerous than the "centers of power" removed May 15, 1971, have made journalism a matter of commerce rather than of principles, and have malformed younger journalists. (BAL pp.24-26)

17 -New arrests reported in Egypt, in army, in labor unions and among students of Alexandria and Assiut. Elections for Alex-

andria and Assiut. Elections for boards of the labor unions to be held soon. (OJ p.12)

18 -Le Monde, citing al-Hurriya of Beirut, reports arrests between the 17th and the 21st of June, of writers, students, lawyers, etc. Four laborers accused of belonging to Communist party. (Le Monde 18/4 p.6; HUR 16/7 p.3)

-Ministry of Higher Education studies the question of granting equivalence to degrees obtained at foreign universities, including American universities in Arab world. Decision to be on purely scientific basis. (AH p.1)

19 -Plan to set up women's "People's Committees" to supervise family-planning program in Manufiya runs into difficulties. Government will set up six "conscientization centers" for family-planning. (AH p.10)

23 -Catholic nuns in Egyptian hospitals among recipients of medals and awards distributed by Sadat. (AH p.4)

-Egyptian companies with Jewish names in their titles have recently changed their titles to all Arabic. (AH p.4)

26 -Cultural relations between Egypt and Britain being restored. Princess Margaret, in her visit to Egypt next fall, will reopen British Council, closed for 16 years. (AH p.1)

27 -On prisons: 1) A secondary industrial school will be established for inmates of men's prison of al-Qanātir al-Kharyriah who have obtained primary certificate. Instruction gratis. (AH 27/7 p.6) 2) Also, 1500 prisoners released early on aniversay of July 23rd Revolution. Their reactions described. (AH 28/7 p.3)

29 -Violent confrontations reported in Cairo between police and people of Sayyadat Zaynab quarter. Occasion was funeral of young man who died in prison. His parents blamed death on police brutality; police say that it was heart attack. (N p.1; NAH p.10)

30 -Dr. A-'Azīz Hijāzī (Min. of Finance and Economics) announced some relaxations: abrogation of all control over foreign commerce; establishment of a free currency exchange market not subject to officially fixed rates; abrogation of need of import licenses for passenger cars. (AH p.1)

-A bureau for family counselling will open in Manufiyah next September to assist personal status courts in preserving and strengthening family ties. (AH p.8)

IV. SYRIA

July
1973

5 -Inauguration of Euphrates Dam today at Tabaqa (name changed to al-Thawra). Throwing a switch, Pres. Hafiz al-Asad diverted the river from the old bed.

-Arab, Rumanian and Soviet delegations attend. Russian delegation included Mr. Andrei Kirilenko, General of Central Committee, Soviet Communist Party. Several speeches on Soviet-Syrian friendship, socialism etc. Pres. al-Asad hailed dam as symbol of liberation and progress, praised Russia's historic friendship for Syria, and warned against Arab defeatism. (N 5/7 p.1; 6/7 p.1,4; YOM 5/7 p.1; 6/7 p.6; SAFA 5/7 p.6; SAFA 6/7 p.1; See also N 24/6 p.4 for Tass article on dam as symbol of Arab-USSR friendship).

-Statistics: dam is 4,500 meters long; will produce 800,000 kilowatts of electricity (MUH 5/7 p.4,5); and over the next 50 years, it will irrigate 1,500,000 fedans of desert land. (YOM 5/7 p.1) Is key to the industrialization of Syria; will form a lake 620 km sq., 11.9 billion cubic meters of water; cost 1.2 billion Syrian pounds (one third was a loan from USSR at 2.5%, to be repaid in 12 years). (BAL p.15; ANB 13/7 p.7). Model villages to be built. (N p.3)

-Imports-exports at Syrian port Tartūs reached 6037 tons during May (4073 tons during April). (YOṀ 5/7 p.1).

NOTE: Increase probably due to tie-up of port of Beirut when Syrian dock-workers left Lebanon after Lebanese Army-Palestinian Resistance clash in May.

10 -Kirilenko (see 5/7) meets Syrian Communist Party leaders, describes efforts to fulfill decisions of Congress on Peace. (N p.1)

11 -A center for Marine Studies, largest in the area, attached to the U. of Latkia, will be set up in Latakia. (HAY p.8)

12 -Lebanese government source denied that Nūr ed-Dīn al-Attāsi sought asylum in Lebanpn; denied Lebanon received such a request. (HAY p.2)

15 -Syria wants Arab capital to invest in Syria in projects the Euphrates dam now makes possible. (NAH p.5)

25 -Opening of Damascus Trade Fair. (N p.4)

V. IRAQ

July
1973

2 -Gen. Hamīd Shihāb (Iraqi Minister of Defense), was killed, and Mr. Sa'dūn Ghaydān (Minister of the Interior), was injured in an abortive coup d'etat on June 30. The leader of the attempt, says the official Iraqi report, was Mr. Nāẓim Kazzār (Chief of the Security). He and his co-conspirators were arrested while trying to flee to Iran. (OJ 2/7 p.1)

-At the obsequies of General Shihāb, Pres. Aḥmad Ḥasan al-Bakr was represented by Mr. Saddām Ḥusayn (Vice-Pres. of the Revolutionary Council). (OJ 3/7 p.12; YOM 4/7 p.6). The Iraqi Communist Party and the Kurdish Democratic Party send condolences to Pres. al-Bakr. (SAFA 6/7 p.1,12)

-For al-Thawra (Baghdad), the foiling of the plot indicates the invincibility of the Ba'th Party, the party of the Arab masses, the paragon of the Arab vanguard. The Revolution was undertaken in the name of the Arab nation, in the interests of millions of proletarians. The success of the Revolution is the proof of its authenticity. (Cited in OJ 3/7 p.12)

-The Arab press speculated on the significance of the plot. al-Ahram (3/7 p.1) saw it the outcome of a split in the Ba'th party leadership. L'Orient-Le Jour (4/7 p.1,6) mentions variant versions: one, that the ultimate target of the coup was Pres. al-Bakr; another sees in the attempt the hand of Gen. Mahdi ᶜAmmāsh (ex-Vice-President, now Iraqi ambassador in Moscow). An editorial in OJ (5/7 p.1) considers the attempt only one stage in vast plot against Iraq by Iran, Jordan and Saudi Arabia. The newspaper of the Kurdish Democratic Party says the Kazzār group was responsible for recent tension between the Kurds and the Iraqi authorities. (SAFA p.1, 12)

7 -Ṣaddām Husayn yesterday told Iraqi Security and Intelligence forces that the mentality of the Security was formed under the old regime; he urged members to educate themselves in the Ba'th party principles. (N 7/7 p.3)

8 -Execution yesterday of Nāẓim Kazzār (Director of Security) and 22 others involved in the June 30 plot, sentenced by special court with Izzat al-Duri (member of Revolutionary Command) presiding.

-Two of the executed were allegedly connected with al-Sa'iqa (Syrian commandos). More sentences are expected. Reports from Baghdad say Abdal-Khaliq al-Samarra'i (member of the regional and national commands), Na'im Haddad (regional command) and Muhammad Fadil (military bureau of the Party) have been arrested. (AH p.1; HAY p.1; N p.4; SAFA p.1; OJ p.1)

9 -Extraordinary meeting of Regional Command of Ba'th Party in Iraq held yesterday. National Command also attended.

-The Regional Command received approval of its action after the June 30 plot and authorization for further action. Expanded Regional Command to be elected within four months and new National Command within six months. (YOM p.1; SAFA p.1,6; HAY p.10)

-Abdal-Khaliq al-Samarra'i and Muhammad Fadil expelled from Party. (NAH p.9)

10 -14 more (including al-Samarra'i and Fadil) sentenced to death for June 30 plot. al-Samarra'i's sentence commuted to life imprisenment. (N p.1; HAY p.1,8; SAFA p.1,12 NAH p.10; AH p.1; YOM p.1)

-All details of the coup as reported from Baghdad. Unforeseen delay in Pres. Bakr's plane from Poland caused the plot to fail. al-Balagh connects plot with recent interview with Barazani (Kurdish leader) published in American press. (9/7 p. 16-18. See also DU S 9/7 p.8-11)

11 -Assistant Military Attaché at Iraqi Embassy in Beirut, in interview, said that the plot indicates Iraqi people wish to be rid of Ba'thist-Takriti dictatorship. Attache has left Beirut for another Arab country. (HAY p.1) Libya granted him asylum. (HAY 12/7 p.1)

12 -Kurdish Democratic Party reported pleased with execution of Kazzar, clemency to al-Samarra'i. (SAFA p.6)

13 -Joseph Chami claims Baghdad, under Russian pressure, is mending differences with Iran.(OJ pp. 1, 12)

-Secret Iraqi-Iranian meeting in Geneva May 7. Kuwait, likely to suffer by this detente, supported Kazzar. (OJ p.1,12)

14 -Revolutionary Command amends the temporary constitution, gives power to President at expense of Revolutionary Command. Pres. Bakr, now President of State, PM, Head of Armed Forces, can exercise executive power directly or through Council of Ministers. (NAH p.1; YOM p.1; and 15/7 N p.1)

-More details of June plot. Iraqi assistant military attaché (al-Mūsawī) in Beirut fled to Libya, was officially summoned to Baghdad three months ago, accused of activities against regime, and imprisoned. During recent events, helped by friends, escaped to Beirut, to Cairo, then to Tripoli (Libya) where he is.

Details given on death of Ḥammad Shihāb after plotters failed to excape; organization of Ba'th party played major role in their capture. Revolutionary Command Council changes provisional constitution, gives Pres. Aḥmad al-Bakr absolute power. He becomes PM and Commander-in-chief, can appoint or dismiss vice-president, ministers, judges, officials, army officers, security men, diplomats. (HAY p.1,8)

Baghdad denied rumors of split in Ba'th leadership, denied that the constitutional changes are aimed at a new stage of development. In press conference Saddām Ḥusayn asserted new National Front will include not only Ba'th and Communist Parties but also Kurdish Democratic Party, and other independent progressive national elements.

(DUS 30/7 p.14; SAY 26/7-2/8 pp.31,32; see also N 29/7 p.1 for text of Central Committee of Iraq Communist Party, issued after meeting held on 27/7, supporting new national front.)

15 -Anniversary celebrations of July 14 (1958) and July 17 (1968) Revolutions begin today.

-al-Yom says, editorially, that the first restored Iraq to a nationalist line, the second gave Iraq its social and economic direction. (p.1)

-Iraq announces "Qasr al-nihaya" (political prison) to be demolished, made into popular park. al-Nahar interprets this and constitutional changes as reconciliatory. (p.1)

16 -Dr. Rashid al-Rifa'i named acting Defense Minister. (YOM p.1)

17 -In Baghdad celebrations, Pres. Bakr announced that autonomy of Iraqi Kurds will be complete by March 1974. (SAFA p.1,12; MUH p.1,12)

18 -Iraqi Ba'th Party formed National Front with Iraqi Communist Party. Two parties jointly announce acceptance of Charter for National Action (announced Nov. 15, 1971). Dialogue with Kurdish Democratic Party continues with aim of incorporating it into Front with other progressive, democratic forces. Law for creation of People's Assembly changed to include 100 members to be selected by Front.
(NOTE: original law dated 1970, but no assembly axists.)
(NAH p.1; SAFA p.12; YOM p.1; also 19/7 YOM p.6, and N p.1)

-Bilal Hasan in al-Balagh reports discussions preceding formation of Front. Communists objected to Ba'th leadership of Front; a compromise formula was found: the parties lead the Front, but Ba'th Party has a special place. Disagreement with Kurds centered on phrase "Iraq is part of Arab nation" in section on Kurds. Phrase was moved to section on Arab problems. Communists proposed two year limit to the exceptional powers of Revolutionary Command; the compromise was that it will be abolished "as quickly as possible". Council of Ministers powers were increased as a result of these discussions. (See above 14/7)

-B. Hasan's article predicts the Front will be led by group of 8 Ba'this, 3 Communists, 3 Kurds, 1 progressive nationalist and 1 independent democrat. People's Assembly will have 150 members (see above 18/7 YOM says 100 members) appointed by Parties in same proportions as the Front. Discussion about composition of Army was excluded. (23/7 p. 6-7)

-In Baghdad National Council for Afro-Asian Peace and Solidarity meets with representatives from So. Yemen, Front for Liberation of Bahrain, and National Peace Committee of So. Yemen. They propose to coordinate action in Gulf and Peninsula with Committee in Baghdad and with Arab and international committees. Parts of declaration given. (N 29/7 p.3)

20 -Report on Baghdad press conference of Saddam Husayn (VP of Revolutionary Command, Deputy Secretary of the Regional Command) concerning the Front and other Arab questions. (N p.1)

(NOTE: See also DUS 16/7 p.40 and BAL 9/7 p.52 on challenges and accomplishments of Iraqi regime.)

29 -Prize to Muḥammad Shukrī Jamil, Iraqi film producer, at 8th world Festival in Moscow for narrative film, al-Ẓāmi'ūn (those who thirst).

VI. JORDAN-PALESTINE

JULY
1973

A. Bourguiba's and Bouteflika's Statements on a Palestinian State

8 -Following Tunisian Pres. Bourguiba's statement to Le Monde (see NAH 3/7 p.9) that a Palestinian state should be set up, that Israel should return to the 1947 frontiers, and that Jordan is an artificially constructed state, Jordan expresses itsastonishment and demands an explanation. (HAY p.1)

11 -George Habash (PFLP) rejects the idea of a Palestinian state as proposed by Zayyāt to the Security Council (see NAH 30/6 p.1) or as proposed by Bourguiba. (NAH p.1)

12 -The Algerian foreign minister Bouteflika, at a press conference in Paris, said that Palestinians would negociate directly with Israelis if Israel expressed its desire to eliminate colonialism. (HAY p.1; NAH p.1; SAFA 13/7 pp.6,12). The Syrian press replies, and also Moshe Dayan. (NAH p.1)

13 -Algerian contacts aimed at creating a Palestine state. Algerian proposals for direct contacts between Palestinians and Israelis. Israeli reactions. The Palestinians (in Damascus) reject the idea. (NAH p.1) Maḥmūd Riyāḍ proposes an Arab summit meeting to resolve the political and military impasse. The Palestinian Resistance should be coordinated and channeled into the general plan. (NAH p.10)

14 -as-Safa (Beirut) editorializes that Bouteflika's statement reflects the political disengagement of the Great Powers, and then of the Arab countries, with regard to Palestine. (SAFA p.1)

-An article by S. Frangie surmises that Egypt wants to promote Aḥmad Chaukeyri again, to set up a Palestinian government in exile. Bourguiba's project is the same as the American Fisher project of 1970. The Resistance is not interested. Husayn would be the victim of the operation. (OJ pp. 1,12)

-Y. Arafāt in Kuweit rejects the Bourguiba project, says 1) Palestinian Revolution will continue to fight for its original goal: a democratic state; 2) the Revolution is not bound by proposals arising from principles outside it; 3) the situation in Lebanon is better than ever before. (N p.1)

-al-Nida' (Communist paper) editorializes against exaggeration of R. Edde's statement that USSR was for a Palestinian state if the Palestinians wanted it. (N p.1)

-To the Jordanian ambassador, Bourguiba clarifies his statement: Jordan is an artificial state. (SAFA p.6)

16 -Discussion of the Palestine state; recent Egyptian and Tunisian views. Discussion of 4 Resistance positions; PDFLP's is most nuanced, but is vague. (BAL pp. 18-21)

17 -Zayyāt says the Palestinians themselves are to decide on a Palestinian state. (NAH p.10)

18 -Jordan cuts diplomatic ties with Tunisia. (N p.1)

-Filastīn al-Thawra, editorially, rejects a Palestinian state on only part of Palestinian land. That the world admits the existence of Palestinian people is in itself a great victory. The Resistance refuses to abandon its arms. (N p.1; NAH p.10)

19 -Libya agrees with Bourguiba that Jordan is an artificial state. (Eban: There is no difference between Palestine and Jordan.) (NAH p.12)

23 -Analysis by Riyāḍ Farḥāt of the struggle between the Hashemites and Bourguibites, critique of their tactics regarding Palestinian state and Israel. (BAL p.4,5)

24 -Y. Arafāt, at a Cairo meeting with Egypt's Press Syndicate, says Palestine Revolution refuses the recent proposals for a Palestine state. (N p.1; see also SAY 26/7-2/8 pp. 28,29 for a discussion of Fath's concept of Palestine state and why it differs from concepts outside the Palestine movement.)

25 -Moshe Dayan admits a Palestinian people but no Palestine; it is part of what is now Jordan. Asserts Israel is now strong enough to disagree with her friends. (NAH p.10)

28 -King Husayn, interviewed by al-Nahār, is not surprised at Bourguiba's views of a Palestinian State in Jordan; Jordan is used to opposition. Relations with Egypt are now excellent. "We cannot help but wish to represent and defend the interests of the Palestinians, if we do not wish the end of the Palestinians and of Palestine". (NAH p.9)

29 -Bourguiba, in Paris, warns that Palestinians without a strategy risk extinction; one solution, the formation of a Palestinian state and a Jewish state. (NAH p.10)

-Y. Arafāt in East Berlin for opening of office for the Palestinian Resistance. (NAH p.12; see also NAH 30/7 p.10; and NAH 4/8 p.10)

B. Bishop Rāyā's Hunger Strike

12 -Joseph Rāyā (Catholic Bishop of Galilee) announces a 3-day fast to be staged in front of the Israeli Parliament in defense of the right of the Christian Arabs of Kafr Bir'am and Iqrit of return to their homes. (MUH p.12; SAFA 16/7 p.6; YOM 16/7 p.1)

17 -Bishop Rāyā begins hunger strike, will prolong it as long as his forces permit. Some farmers join. He will organize a group prayer tomorrow. (SAFA p.6; N p. 1; AH p.1)

19 -400-500 hunger strikers before Parliament. (SAFA p.6; AH p.1)

C. Miscellaneous

8 -Meeting of Communist youth in al-Tība (Israel), demanding withdrawal of occupying forces and rights for Arabs. (N p.1)

9 -Iraq newspaper says Druze armed resistance against Israel is continuing. (YOM p.6)

10 -Arafāt meets al-Asad in Damascus. First time Arafāt has

left Beirut publicly (he visited al-Asad secretly before) since the May incidents. (HAY p.1)

11 -Commemoration at Arab U., Beirut, of first anniversary of the death of Ghassān Kanafāni. Jumblatt calls on the national forces and Arab peoples to defend the cause of the Palestinians. Habash (PFLP) rejects any deviation from the aims of war of liberation, revolutionary strategy; rejects Bourguiba's solution; says the existence of the revolution in Lebanon is necessary; asserts the Lebanese masses defended the Resistance in May.

Lebanese press leader Riyād Ṭāha replied that the Lebanese people were defending their own land, nationality, and history. (MUH p.12; YOM pp.1,6; HAY p.10; N p.1; N 12/7 p.3)

14 -Copy of the Quran dating back to the Ayyūbī era (13th century A.D.) was found in excavations of a mosque in al-Salṭ (30 km west of Amman). (HAY p.8)

-Secretary of the Communist Party in Israel forbidden to enter Israeli parliament dining hall because she wore a mini-skirt. Also in parliament, speakers protested against summer camps which mix Arabs and Jews, as encouraging intermarriage. (HAY p.8)

-In a letter to <u>al-Hayat</u>, ᶜAbd al-Raḥmān Murād, member of the Palestinian National Council, responds to an article of 5/7 entitled, "A New Split in the Liberation Front", in which his name was mentioned. Murad denies he favored the Front's continued existence after it was to be included in Fath; says no new command should be named; the Palestinian ranks should be unified, not split. (HAY p.3)

15 -President of Jordan Federation of Benevolent Ass'ns complains to UN that Israel plans to abolish the Fed. in Jerusalem and the West Bank, and to attach the Ass'ns to government agencies. (SHIH p.2)

18 -Report on Israeli obliteration of Arab villages; purpose to obliterate history of the Arabs and their sanctuaries. (MUH p.10)

20 -Syndicate of Electrical Workers in Jordan protests to Ministry of Labor dismissal of people from syndicate by authorities in collaboration with intelligence. (N p.1)

-393 Gaza students at Egyptian schools cross the canal, under supervision of International Red Cross, to visit families. (AH p.10)

-Analysis by ᶜUthmān ᶜUthmān of Communist class struggle and the national struggle for liberation as applied to Palestine revolution. (MUH p.11 and 21/7 p.11)

25 -Israeli court sentences 10 Palestinians seized in Lebanon. The defense denies validity of the sentence. (NAH p.10)

-WAFA (Palestinian Agency) condemns the hijacking of Japanese air liner by organization called "Sons of the Occupied Territories". (NAH p.1; see also NAH 29/7 p.1 for Libyan condemnation of the hijacking and 31/7 p.1 for PFLP's denial of any part in it.)

27 -Tract distributed in Beirut (source unknown) from the "Sons of the Occupied Territories": states the Japanese jet was hijacked in reprisal for Japanese indemnity to Israel of 6 million dollars for Japanese terrorist attack on Lod Airport in May, 1972. (NAH p.1)

31 -Protests in Palestine Refugee camp Burj al-Shamālī in Tyre over lack of water, medicine, doctors and bad supervision of food distribution. On Monday 2/8 10,000 Palestinians demonstrate; they cut off reception of food, stopped all UNRWA services, and criticized UNRWA and the rich Arab countries for not giving aid. (N p.3; NAH 2/8 p.3; BAL 6/8 pp.12-13; AH 4/8 p.1)

VII. THE ARABIAN PENINSULA AND THE GULF

JULY
1973

Oman:

22 -Declarations of Student Federations in Bahrain on events in Gulf and Oman: secret trials, torture, etc. Telegram sent to Arab League by Fed. of Arab students. (N p. 3)

Saudi Arabia

8 -UN announces S. Arabia has joined 2 intl. treaties (1926 and 1957) against slavery. (HAY p.8)

-King Faysal says it will be difficult to continue close cooperation with US if US does not change its position on Palestine.

14 -Radio Aden announces that S. Arabia has sentenced 135 people (military and civilian) to death, 305 to life imprisonment, 752 to prison terms of 10-15 years, for belonging to some nationalist organizations. (N p.1)

24 -Experts from Islamic states meet in Jedda to elaborate basic principles for an Islamic Bank, whose creation was approved March 1972 at meeting of For. Ministers of Islamic countries. (SAFA p.4)

Yemen

10 -No. Yemen announces pardon for all rebels who turn themselves in. (HAY p.8)

11 -No. Yemen announces clash with band of saboteurs; its leader is killed. Arms and important papers seized. Gvt. accuses So. Yemen of financing saboteurs. (HAY p.8)

12 -PM al-'Iriyani (No. Yemen) says only one island belonging to Yemen is occupied by foreign forces. That island is Abu ^{c}Ali, occupied by British in 1968 when they withdrew from the Gulf. (HAY p.8)

13 -People's Court in Aden condemns 7 to death for spying for Oman and S. Arabia. (N.p.1)

30 -Article with brief history of political developments in Yemen since 1967. (BAL pp. 24-26)

VIII. NORTH AFRICA

JULY
1973

ALGERIA

8 -7th Encounter of Islamic Thought at Tizi-Ouzou, 10-20/7. Dr. A. Aziz Kāmil (Vice-Premier for Religious Affairs and Minister of Awqaf) reads a message from Sadat. In the Egyptian delegation is Sheikh Muh. al-Ghazali (Dir. Gen. of the Ministry of Awqaf). (AH p.1; see also AH 9/7 p.4)

Members of the Lebanese delegation from Dar al-Ifta': Prof. Hussein al-Quwatli(DG of Ifta' Affairs) Shaikh Taha al-Sabunji (Sharia judge of Akkar), Dr. 'Umar Farrūkh. (YOM p.4). Also Fathi Yakin (editor of Shihab)representing the Islamic Associations, "al-jama^c at al-islamiyah", of Lebanon. (SHIH 15/7 p.2) Agenda: problems facing the Muslim world, including measures to be taken against the imperialism of missionaries. (HAY 12/7 p.8)

Short play of Taha al-'Amiri (Dir. of Algerian National Theatre) who is passing through Beirut. (BAL 9/7 pp. 48-9)

-The Algerian press announces that in 1975 all the laws dating from the French period will have been annulled. (YOM p.7)

30 -al-Balagh (30/7 pp. 22-23) recounts Pres. Boumedien's talks with the 3,000 students to go through the country to explain the revolution and see if laws on nationalization of the land are being applied. He suggested that the past tense be dropped from their language; they must forget about their ancestors and focus on what they can do, now. He announced that health services will be free beginning in January; also that new "basic schools" of 9 years will be begun to solve the problem of students who find the 6th primary a block.

LIBYA

3 -Libyan government to facilitate passport formalities for countries agreeing to use Arabic on passports of nationals wishing to visit Libya. Number of countries is 24, including Turkey, West Germany, Britain and Italy. (AH 23/6 p.2; SAFA 2/7 p.6; AH 3/7 p.1) Belgium, Luxemburg, Austria. (AH 9/7 p.5) Number is 33, Radio Libya says, including Norway and Rumania. (AH 30/1 p.1)

4 -Fedayin training bases in Libya have been closed. Some Palestinians expelled from Libya. 13,000 Palestinians live in Libya, some 5,000 of them teachers. (OJ p.1) Report of expulsion of Palestinians in Libya denied by PLO in Tunis. (SAFA 5/7 p.6)

9 -"USSR and Mu'ammar al-Qadhdhafi"; discussion of a Soviet article concerning Qadhdhafi's positions on communism and socialism. (AH p.5)

-"The story of Qadhdhafi's flight to Cairo": 3 pages on serious tensions within Libyan Revolutionary Command. (DUS p.12)

-International conference of Islamic youth, opened at Tripoli on 7/7. 2-day discussion of the Third Theory of the word (Islam). One speaker said that the Quran has not annulled nationalities but parties. (HAY p.8)

-Conference sends a telegram to world Islamic leaders on Muslim minorities oppressed in Russia, China, Bulgaria, Albania. It expresses its concern for the Pakistani prisoners of war in India and asks Arab leaders to intervene for them. (HAY 11/7 p.8)

-Conference condemns the Islamic states which deal with Israel. (YOM 13/7 p.1)

-Conference composed of 98 delegates including one from the Lebanese league of Muslim students. (SHIH 15/7 p.2)

12 -Competition organized for design of a "national Islamic" uniform; prize of 45,000 dinars. (SAFA p.12; HAY p.8)

15 -Popular committees ask for the replacement of 4 foreign embassies in Tripoli which are too close to the port and the sea. (SAFA p.6) Libya and Tunisia are ready to sign an accord for a common organization of the press and distribution. (YOM p.6)

-Bashir Huwādī (Sec. Gen. of Libyan ASU) tells students who go abroad: practice Islam to make it better known, beware of material and immoral Western civilization; secularism tries to separate politics and divine law, thinking that science is everything; but Islam says that science is only one of the ways of knowing.(YOM p.8)

17 -400 communists or atheists, mainly intellectuals and technocrats, arrested in Libya in 15 days. (SAFA p.6, citing Figaro Paris).

21 -Egyptian-Libyan cooperation for construction in Libya. (AH p.7)

22 -Demonstrations, telegrams to Qadhdhafi to withdraw his resignation. (AH p.1)

23 -Unless Col. Qadhdhafi withdraws resignation, Revolutionary Command Council and Government of Libya will both resign. (NAH p.10; SAFA pp. 1,6; AH p.1)

-PM Abdal-Salam Jaloud on March on Egypt: "The masses did what we could not succeed in doing for four years, they broke down the barriers between Libya and Egypt". (AH p.1)

-Egyptians resident in Libya march to Qadhdhafi's headquarters, demand he withdraw resignation. (AH p.1)

24 -Col. Qadhdhafi, in a 3-hour radio talk at Benghazi, withdraws resignation, will stay as President until the inevitable union with Egypt is completed; describes Egypt as

"corruption, censorship, bureaucracy... Egypt needs a popular revolution". (AH p.1; SAFA p.12; N p.1)

26 -Article in al-Ahram by Jamal al-[c]Utayfi on "The Experiment of People's Committees in Libya". He discussed the question with participants in Libyan "unity march" last week and discovered that most of the advantages claimed for Popular Revolution in Libya are already laid out in ASU National Charter in Egypt. In Charter these advantages are sought in framework of the sovereignty of law; many are being achieved already in Egypt. (p.7)

29 -Revolutionary Command Council calls workers in hospitals (doctors, nurses, workers) to seize power in their sector. (SAFA p.12)

30 -High-jackers of JAL Jumbo will be judged according to Islamic law, may receive the death sentence or have an arm or leg cut off. (NAH p.1; also YQM 2/8 p.6; NAH 4/8 p.10)

MOROCCO

9 -Trials at Quneitra. Details on the accused. (DUS p.15; BAL pp. 20-23). BAL publishes letter of Prof. Julian from Le Monde.

10 -Property of 2 factories turned over to workers. Project for mobilization of youth for 2 years for national service. (HAY p.8)

17 -All the Moroccan military force arrives in Syria. (SAFA p.6)

TUNISIA

14 -Article of F. Jabre on Aboul Kassem al-Chabi (Tunisia) on the printing of his unpublished poems. (SAFA 14/7 p.9)

17 -Opening of the Pan-African Festival of Youth in Tunis 15/7; 30 countries, 3,500 participants, including Palestine Resistance. (SAFA p.6)

EGYPT ON THE EVE OF WAR: DIALOGUE AND NATIONAL UNITY

by JOHN J. DONOHUE, S.J. and SHEREEN KHAIRALLAH

The "self-criticism" generated in the Arab world by the trauma of June 1967 was bound to bring political and ideological changes which would be new attempts to solve the persistent problems of development. Simultaneously some of the old divisions patched up or brushed aside by the wave of revolution and the influence of charism began to appear again. Egypt has appeared to be the country most sensitive to the actions and reactions set in train by June 1967. The tension between its Arabness and its Egyptianness appeared no way reduced by the years of self-assumed leadership of the Arab revolution and of Arab socialism. In fact, there seemed to be a tendency since the war of 1967 to focus on Egyptian national problems and on Egyptian cultural traits while downplaying Egypt's role as the spearhead of the Arab revolution. At the same time, the release of the Muslim Brothers and the removal of more doctrinaire Marxist elements from the A.S.U. marked an attempt to establish a new meld of the old and the new which was caught up in Sadat's slogan of "faith and science".

Student strikes supported by some intellectuals, and the expulsion of journalists from the A.S.U. exposed the tensions in Egyptian society under Pres. Sadat in the state of "no war, no peace".

It was in this situation that Pres. Sadat proposed and organized a Dialogue for National Unity within the framework of the political institutions. At the time, "Dialogue" appeared little more than a saving slogan covering up a rather forceful muffling of some of the more eloquent spokesmen in Egytian society. But that was before October.

October may not have changed everything, but it surely does cast a different light on Sadat and his dialogue. Was the dialogue a distraction and a stalling? Or was it a preparation for the war? Or conversely, was the war the goad to push the dialogue along Sadat's chosen course? Such questions easily come to mind. The answers demand information difficult of access. Still, a review of the articles on the dialogue which appeared in August and September in al-Ahram may offer some bits of information which can be pieced together with subsequent developments to form an answer.

THE CALL FOR DIALOGUE

One aspect of Pres. Sadat's style of governing has been his consultation of various sectors of the population. For instance, in 1971 the redaction of the new Constitution was preceded by discussion on a rather broad basis.[1] But in early 1973 the theme of dialogue was coming from other quarters. Ahmad Baha al-Din asked for dialogue to resolve the conflicting currents of thought which were rending Egypt. (AH 21/1/73 p.5). The conflict centered around the real content of Nasserism. Sadat's theme, at the time, was "the deviation of the reactionary right and the adventurist left", and the "sovereignty of the law". Baha al-Din and several other journalists were expelled from the Arab Socialist Union (A.S.U.). One cause cited was that an earlier and limited "dialogue" produced a demand for a multi-party system and a free press in Egypt.[2] However, the theme of dialogue was restored by an article of Tawfiq al-Hakim after his rehabilitation in June 1973.[3]

Pres. Sadat took up the theme in a meeting with the Central Committee of the A.S.U. on July 16 in which he proposed the analysis and study of the effect of the international detente on Egypt and the Middle East. A paper was in preparation which would be presented to the Central Committee of the A.S.U. and to the National Congress. The paper would define Egypt's position for the next 20 or 25 years. He also announced that an ideological paper would be prepared to explain the Charter in such a way as to avoid interpretations which were in opposition to the Charter, deviating to Marxism. Explanations must be based on the reality of the present including the changes which have taken place. The paper could not be ready for the National Congress scheduled for July 23. (The Congress would be postponed to September.) Besides Sadat wished that the subject of this paper (or papers) be the subject of a wide national dialogue on all levels before the paper took its final form which would define the frame for Egypt's movements for the next 25 years. This dialogue would be in the frame of "our basic political institutions".
(AH 17/7/73 pp. 1,7)

SADAT'S JULY 23, 1973 SPEECH

In his speech on the anniversary of the 1952 Revolution, July 23, Sadat set forth the theme of changed conditions: the form of the meeting is different this year; we need something new: deep thought to realize our demands in a situation very different from what we and the world lived in since the beginning of the Revolution till now. Even though some land is occupied, things are completely different, due to the Revolution. "If we ask ourselves why, after 6 years we have not achieved what we sought... it is because conditions around us have changed and we still have not grasped the effect of these changes". The remedy he suggested was that the Central Committee and the People's Assembly share with him in thinking and planning and in organizing the widest possible dialogue including all the forces of the people in a free and open discussion.

It should be noted that the discussion or dialogue was not to touch the ideological basis, the question of what is Nasserism. That would be defined in a separate paper. As Sadat said in his speech of Oct. 16, 1973, he was not interested in wasting time on sterile ideological discussion. Rather, the discussion would be realistic -- the changes in world conditions and the influence of the changes on the Egyptian and Arab situation.

Two days after the speech, the special committee formed to prepare the working paper and set up the dialogue began meeting under the chairmanship of Hafiz Badawi, Pres. of the People's Assembly. (AH 26/7/73 p.1). The country was divided into six groupings: Cairo, Alexandria, Giza, and Minya (each with surrounding areas) plus a special grouping for Universities, Research Centers and Judicial Organizations and another for Workers and Professional Unions along with Youth Organizations[4]. Officials were appointed to administer the dialogue in each of the six areas. Also arrangements were made to hold open sessions in the People's Assembly to hear any citizen who wished to contribute. (AH 27/7/73 p.1)

THE WORKING PAPER

On August 4 the Joint Congress of the Central Committee and the People's Assembly met to hear and discuss the working paper presented by Dr. Rif^{c}at Mahjūb, Secretary of Propaganda and Thought. al-Ahram printed the presentation. (AH 5/8/73 p.5)

Dr. Mahjūb recounted the changes on the national and Arab scene since the Charter. The Corrective Movement of May 15,1971 which returned the July Revolution to its correct path by setting up agencies and establishing freedoms along with the sovereignty of law marked a new stage. At the same time the world scene witnessed important political, economic, technical, social and moral changes. New economic and political forces appeared, leading to political and economic mergers as detente brought the cold war to an end. This change in the objective conditions demands national action which follows these changes, continually examining solutions and policies. Re-examination is not retreat -- the documents of the revolution and its goals remain. Still those responsible must guarantee new policies to face change while bearing in mind that relations among states are drawn up on the basis of their national interests.

But what are the changes that demand new policy? As set out by Dr. Mahjūb they are:

1) political: US-Russian detente, US-Chinese relations, West Germany's relations with E. Germany, Poland, Czechoslovakia and Russia and the end of the Vietnam War. In addition, Arab oil producing countries have begun to appear as a force with influence in the world of energy and money. Africa has begun to show its importance.

2) economic: world wide economic openness shows that economic considerations override ideological differences... socialist countries are open to foreign investment. Also there is a world energy and monetary crisis.

3) technological: evolution in means of production in advanced countries is widening the gap separating them from poor countries. The advance in production of weapons, even conventional weapons, is singled out, with the concurrent phenomenon of limited wars.

4) social and moral: the above changes have had an effect in social relations and conduct, causing anxiety and confused vision especially among some youth. Also there is the population explosion and the brain drain.

The detente has had some negative effects. It has made the U.S. more daring in its support of Israel and enmity to Arabs, leading it to block the way to a just political solution. It has weakened the U.N. It has subjected the Middle East to the strategy of the Super Powers, e.g. the USSR allowing emigration for Israel. Finally, it has made Egypt's reliance on outside forces less active and more limited. The response is obvious: keep old friends, make new friends, be open to all forces while guarding neutrality and relying on one's own (Egyptian and Arab) force.

The military response must be a revivification of the Eastern Front, a search for new sources of arms and the establishment of Arab arms manufacture. The economic response is more openness between Arab economies and encouragment of the private sector of the national economy.

In Dr. Mahjūb's words: "To be very clear, it is not possible to expose to danger the destiny of the battle, a future of new construction and our daily bread for the sake of adolescent ideology or contentions between schools of thought".

He then gives a summary of matters requiring attention. On the national level: clarification of the ideological line of the July 23 Revolution is needed to prevent deviation; the new Egyptian man must be built in a way which guards Egyptian moral, religious and national values and guarantees the building of a modern state; we must strengthen our economic capacity for war and construction; we must establish scientific administration and economic openness.

On the Arab level, a positive atmosphere must replace the negative in work for Arab unity; Arab oil and capital must be used for Arab interests, dangers in the Gulf must be faced, the Eastern Front must be opened, and support must be given to the Arab League, the Tripartite Federation and Libyan-Egyptian unity.

On the international level, all relations must be defined in terms of joint interests and the position of a country with regard to Arab rights; African ties must be strengthened; the U.N. efforts in the M.E. must be supported, and the styles for practicing neutrality in the stage of detente must be found.

The paper was discussed and finally approved for distribution. At the meeting Dr. Hafiz Ghanim, First Secretary of the Central Committee, announced that a special ideological document on the specific characteristics of Arab socialism, and its accord with economic openness has been prepared as well as two other working papers, one on foreign policy, the other on Arab policy.

One point which appears to underlie the working paper is the necessity of idelogical disengagement in order to allow pragmatic and independent action.[5] This disengagement has repercussions on all levels. On the national level it shunts off ideological discussion and allows economic openness; on the Arab level it puts an end to the old Nasserite division of Arab countries into "progressive" and "reactionary" and on the international level it allows Sadat and the Arabs to set their own course whether it be war or the use of Arab oil and capital.

Sadat's consciousness that the international situation was ripe for independent Arab action was clear in the July 23 speech:

> "We find the Arab area a force capable of making an impression on the economies of the world... This area is rich and strategic both politically and economically... We can exert influence... active and constructive influence... the energy crisis and the monetary crisis are our keys... we can have influence... what we need is more mobilization". (AH 24/7/73)

The exercise of that influence by independent action would only be hampered by ideological restraints.

The reaction that the "working paper" provoked among one sector of the Egyptian intellectuals is exemplified in the articles by Ghali Shukri, living in self-imposed exile in Beirut. In two articles in the Beirut weekly al-Balagh entitled "The full story on the documents of 23 July" and "The working paper: from re-examination to retreat", he reviewed the philosophy of the Egyptian revolution as it came to be embodied in the Charter and the Declaration of March 3, and the consequent revision of the ideology under Sadat. He claims that the common element shared by the new faces who formed Sadat's policy was their religious ideology. (BAL, Aug. 20,1973 pp. 29-38; Aug. 27, pp. 29-34)

THE DIALOGUE

The dialogue started in earnest in the second week of August and received rather full coverage in al-Ahram. The following chronology gives an idea of the frequency and tenor of the meetings:

9/8 -Dialogue Meeting of representatives of Judicial Organizations and university and research communities. Dr. H. Ghanim spoke underlining the fact that Egypt is not changing its commitment to socialism, freedom and unity. Discussion of economic openness, detente, science and technology in Egypt's future.

10/8 -Teachers' and Doctors' Unions meet for dialogue. Suggestions: give people full information on the political situation, stop graft and routine; people's march for unified Arab stand; ask the USSR to fulfill its agreements.

11/8 -Teachers' Union dialogues on the building of the Egyptian man. Too much deviation from socialism; deviation of press and media; religious values.

14/8 -Peasant leadership meets with Dr. Ghanim and Mr. Badawi at A.S.U.

15/8 -Open dialogue at People's Assembly yesterday. Suggestions: unify all the documents of the Revolution in one Charter to define the ideological line for the future; remove "the new class" which is isolated from masses and from leaders. A student expressed astonishment that Egypt after 7000 years is still searching for an ideology; scratch the earth of Egypt and you will find its ideology.

-Professional Unions also met.

16/8 -Women's Organizations held dialogue meeting.

-Another open session at People's assembly. A journalist demanded guarantees to allow people to express opinions without fear. A citizen suggested a suicide phalange of 10,000 youths to hurl themselves at enemy positions. Another asked for a frank explanation of the 1967 set-back.

19/8 -Another popular meeting to discuss the working paper. Dr. Ghanim: our principles are in touch with nationalism, religion and thought.

21/8 -Meeting of Youth Organizations for dialogue. Suggestions: strengthen political structures and foster democracy, economic legislation in accord with Revolution and with present changes. Dr. Utayfi: foreign investment will strengthen national development and will not weaken public sector.

22/8 -Student leadership discusses working paper: scientific approach to problems of youth; invite foreign investment.

23/8 -A suggestion committee of A.S.U. will collect suggestions for submission to joint A.S.U.- People's assembly meeting next month.

30/8 -Administrative Board of Central Federation of Agriculture and Cooperatives, representing 25 million peasants, dialogues: abolish graft, introduce electricity and modern machinery, restudy import restrictions, expand industry outside cities.

-Youth at Qalyubia: hold to principles of July 23 Revolution and to religious and spiritual values.

-1000 Shaikhs and village magistrates meet. Recommend fire-fighting teams in all villages.

31/8 -Dialogue meeting in Alexandria of Christian and Muslim religious leaders. Dr. Abdul-Aziz Kamil, Minister of State for Religious Affairs, spoke: the Egyptian form of socialism has destroyed the myth of the alienation of socialist thought from religion; socialism assures national unity based on tolerance transcending barriers of confessional fanaticism; religious education and research can contribute to the increase of science and faith.

-Meeting in Aswan. Mr. Badawi: Egypt is the graveyard of aggressors; the Arab nation will revive its past. Suggestion: construction of new Egyptian man on religious and ethical bases.

1/9 -Young Men's Muslim Association at Qena meets. Asks for

clarification of July 23 ideology, construction of new man in such a way that religious, ethical and national values are preserved; openness to outside world and support of Palestinians.

-The Federation of Industries will discuss the working paper, especially the points on: freedom and socialism, mixed economy and encouragement of private sector; ethical and social education for constructing the new man; use of Arab oil and capital in the battle.

7/9 -Dialogue meeting at Kafr al-Shaikh: education; use of media for religious training and for erasing illiteracy; economic openness.

8/9 -Dialogue Committee of People's Assembly will set aside five days, beginning Sept. 15, to hear opinions on scientific and technological progress, Arab self-sufficiency and foreign relations.

16-18/9 - Arab intellectuals hold a three-day session on dialogue in People's Assembly. Lebanese speakers: Kamal Shatila (Lebanese Nasserite Organization), Deputy Najāh Wakīm, and Wafiq Tibi (Lebanese editor and V.P. of Fed. of Arab Journalists). George Sidqi (Syrian Ba'th) objected to putting U.S.A. and U.S.S.R. on the same side vis-à-vis the Arabs. A speaker demands abolishing press censorship. Strong reactions to the alternatives presented by Dr. Hilmi Mūrad, former Minister of Education:

1) war now; 2) freeze situation while developing economic and military strength; or 3) surrender.

19/9 -The National Congress of A.S.U. will be postponed till after ᶜId al-Fitr (late October) to allow time for proper preparation of the report on the dialogue.

20/9 -Parliamentary Committee listens to suggestions: priorities in scientific research, research grants only to deserving students, time-limit for eradicating illiteracy.

PRESS ESSAYS

Concurrently with the dialogue meetings, al-Ahram carried a series of articles by various authors giving their reflections on points in the working paper. These essays fall roughly into two categories: economic openness and cultural progress.

ECONOMIC OPENNESS

The articles on economics, as one would expect, advocate economic openness while guarding Egyptian socialism.

Thus, Fayiqa ᶜAbdu (AH 10/8 p.6) discussed the scientific and technological guidelines of the working paper, saying that science and technology must be tied to the socio-economic situation. Egypt must work on a national as well as an international scale to catch up with the modern age. Two articles by Jamal al-ᶜUtayfi (AH 16/8 p.5 and 23/8 p.5) also spoke of the new policy of economic openness, which does not contradict socialism. By studying precedents in Russia and other socialist countries, he decided that foreign investment was compatible with socialism, and that one must take advantage of this. Faruq Juwayda (AH 17/8 p.7) talked about Arab economic integration and the problems of the modern age. An interview with Dr. Abdul-Aziz Hijazi, Minister of Finance and Economics (AH 19/8 p.5), on the new economic policy and international changes mentioned in President Sadat's working paper, concluded that this policy was not a deviation from socialism, but on the contrary, the strengthening of socialism.

Ibrahim Nafi^c (AH 26/8 p.5) emphasized the need for flexibility, and said that the importation of certain items needed for development would eventually lead to the socialization of wealth. Development, for ^cAla' al-Din Hilal (AH 28/8 p.5), is in the importance of modern tools and techniques; social justice is the essence of development, as is progress in social attitudes; development is also the modernization of political structures. All these are inter-connected, but must have a common denominator to unify them.

A. Mun'im al-Bara (AH 15/9 p. 5) spoke about the manifestations and constituents of economic openness. The new policy, necessary owing to the changed relations between the super powers, is a logical consequence of non-alignment. It does not clash with the politico-economic structures of a country, but on the contrary, is consistent with Egyptian socialism, which, in effect, is the sharing in all good things. The international changes which have occurred were also the subject of Jamal al-^cUtayfi's article (AH 20/9 p.5); he also mentioned the use of petroleum as an arm in the international struggle against Israel.

THE NEW EGYPTIAN MAN

The building of the new Egyptian man was a very minor point in the working paper. The theme is not new; it has been a preoccupation for several decades. How to become modern and still keep one's cultural identity. For most it is a delicate balance between authenticity and openness, but the content of each element varies with the ideological bias of the author. Here is a sample of the articles of al-Ahram on this theme.

Zaki Najib Mahmūd (AH 6/8 p.5) discussed the opening of Egypt to modern thought which took place from the time of Bonaparte's Egyptian campaign (1798), and the difficulties experienced in combining Western ideas with traditional ones. Although the Revolution opened the doors to modern thought, it must be recast in an Egyptian mould, not adopted helter-skelter. Najib Matar (AH 7/8 p.5) spoke about three different cultures: the culture of the street, the culture of the people, and the culture of the age. The latter two eventually merge -- for the culture of the people is a true one -- to form a world culture. But one must beware of the culture of the street, which is temporary, and founded on bigotry and the seeming problems of the moment.

The inevitability of change and progress in all sectors of human activity was the subject of Salah Tahir (AH 10/8, p.5). Fear of the new is not restricted to Egypt; but the need for innovation is necessary, in order to catch up with the modern age.

In the same vein, but from a more particular view point, al-Sayyid Yasin (AH 17/8 p.7) criticized the Arab mentality. To understand Arab backwardness, a study of the environment is necessary. In other words, socio-economic history, which gave rise to a certain mentality, must be studied in order to correct this mentality.

"How to improve the pulse of our nation?". al-Sayyid Ahmad (AH 22/8 p.5) felt this could be accomplished by catching up with modern times. The Arab world talks about "awakening", but it is far better to begin with an open mind, in order to improve the inherent defects in society. Through knowing what is needed, and through action, people will waken to the realization that it is up to them, not to the government, to act.

Isolation in the midst of the crowd (AH 20/8 p. 5) was the subject of Zaki Najib Mahmūd's article. He spoke of two different kinds of isolation. The isolation which comes from psychological deficiency must be rejected. However, the isolation of thinkers is necessary and constructive. These people, by their very silence, by neither agreeing nor disagreeing, manage to point out the ills of society.

The same writer (AH 29/8 p.5) discussed politics: politicians pursued goals and values instilled by society. But in planning for the new Arab man, the future, not the past, must be taken into consideration. A living society rejects old and useless traditions, and adopts new and helpful ways.

The naive outlook of the Arabs in their reaction towards modern culture was compared by Zaki Najib Mahmud (AH 17/9 p.5) to that of Don Quixote. al-Sayyid Yasin (AH 18/9 p.5), returning to the theme of the new Arab man, discussed how he was to be formed. Socialists say this is possible, for man's personality is determined by his enviroenment. The new man's main characteristic is openness. Therefore what is needed is a revolution in ways of thinking and in social and economic structures, again within socialism. At the same time, socialism does not deny or neglect man's spiritual needs in favour of the merely material.

al-Sayyid Ghalab (AH 29/9 p.7) feels that the search for roots and modernization can be carried out within the framework of Islam, which is not only a religion, but a whole civilization as well. If medieval Muslim man, faced with the same problems as Egyptians today, could rise above them to create a powerful and living culture, so can modern man.

CONCLUSION

Further dialogue meetings had been scheduled for October, but the launching of war on October 6th put an end to discussion and translated the dialogue into action. The articles in al-Ahram continued but the tone changed. There was no longer question of building the new Egyptian man - he was born in crossing the canal on October 6th.[7]

The press reports on the national dialogue illustrate how the political agencies of Egypt can be mobilized to disseminate a theme. The dialogue was not action-oriented, it was a call to think together. It was a sort of "mobilization and concentration", to borrow a phrase of Sadat. The question that immediately comes to mind is: how much effect such mobilization of political agencies actually has on the thinking of the people as a whole. In the context of Egypt before October 1973, the dialogue must have appeared as a slightly new form to an old ritual. Some of the opinions expressed in the dialogue meetings indicate as much. The democratic freedoms restored by Sadat's Corrective Movement reguired careful control. That along with economic problems and the state of "no war, no peace" did not offer the best situation for bridging the "credibility gap" between the government and the people.

But it would be wrong to look on the dialogue as a mere tactic for distraction while Sadat waited to choose the opportune moment for war. The dialogue and its documents have meaning only in the frame of a very deliberate and organized effort by Sadat and several around him to establish a new legitimacy for the regime which followed Nasir. This appears more clearly now as the motivation for Sadat's complete rebuilding of the A.S.U. from the base to the summit after May 15, 1971 and the subsequent "Program for National Action". It has been pointed out that the "Working Paper" contained nothing that is not found in the speeches of Sadat on the occasions of the expulsion of the Russian experts, the student troubles, and the expulsion of the writers and journalists from the A.S.U. What was new was that the presentation of these ideas in the "working paper" for widespread dialogue added a quality of "legitimacy" to the new directions Sadat chose to take.[8]

June 1967 was a turning point in the Arab world. The period of "revolution" had outlived its usefulness. As one Egyptian official remarked: Nasir died in June 1967.[8] Sadat had the burden of breaking out of established slogans and patterns to establish a new ground for action oriented more to the future than to the charismatic past. The dialogue was an essential stage in the process which started in May 1971. The October War was its climax.

Notes:

1. See Joseph P. O'Kane, "Islam in the new Egyptian constitution", Middle East Journal, 26 (1972) N° 2, pp. 137-148.

2. See Ghali Shukri, "The full story on the documents of 23 July", al-Balāgh, 20/8/1973, p. 37.

3. See translation of Hakim's article in CEMAM Reports, 1 (Sept. 1973) N° 2, pp. 91-101.

4. These are the divisions of the Arab Socialist Union.

5. See the article of Fathi Radwan calling for a cessation of ideology, al-Ahram 4/2/1973, p.5

6. Note: the dates given are the dates when the discussions were reported in al-Ahram.

7. For a treatment of the war literature on the theme of the new Arab man, see the article on pp. 23-36 of this volume.

8. G. Shukri, al-Balagh, 20/8/73, p. 38.

9. See interview with Husayn al-Shafi'i, entitled "Jamal Abdel-Nasser died in 1967", al-Hawadith, 27/7/73, pp. 18-20.

ṬĀHĀ ḤUSAYN (1889-1973)

by Robert B. Campbell, S.J.

"His death brings to a close a volume in the history of Egypt", wrote Lūwīs ᶜAwad recently, "a massive volume millions have read over four generations". (AH 29/10 p.5). For the entire Arab world, Egyptians most of all, the death, last October 29, 1973, of Ṭāhā Ḥusayn, the dean of Arab letters, just short of his 84th birthday, meant more than the passing of a great literary figure. It was the end of an era, which Dr. Zakī Najīb Maḥmūd[1] does not hesitate to call "the era of Ṭāhā Ḥusayn". (AH 30/10 p.5).

Coinciding with the cease-fire of the October war, an event of considerable political, economic, and psychological significance for the Arabs, the passing of Ṭāhā Ḥusayn has been spoken of as related, symbolically, to the changes the war has brought about. Dr. Muhammad Anīs[2] compares his death with that of another great Egyptian literary figure al-Manfalūṭī, who died in 1924 the very day an effort was made to halt the liberation movement by an attempt on the life of Saᶜd Zaghlūl, the za'īm al-Ummah (leader of the nation). At al-Manfalūṭī's funeral, Ahmad Shawqī, Egypt's great poet, referred to this event in his elegy:

> "You have chosen a day of shock as a day of farewell
> The news of your death has come in the midst of a violent storm".

Dr. Anīs applies these words to Ṭāhā Ḥusayn "who died in the midst of the people's struggle against the enemy, while news of that struggle gripped every ear and heart". (AH 30/10 p.5). "His soul departed from this life after despair departed from the soul of Egypt", said Tawfiq al-Ḥakīm in his eulogy at the funeral of Ṭāhā Ḥusayn. (AH 1/11 p.8).

Hence, the death of this great literary figure, who is portrayed as symbolizing much of what the Egyptians and Arabs have been struggling for, has occured at a moment which is crucial for the Arabs and which has provoked a flood of commentary and reflection on themselves. The many articles, reminiscences, and studies on Ṭāhā Ḥusayn that have appeared in Arabic newspapers and periodicals seem, then, to be a reflection of the Arabs on themselves, as well as a tribute to one of their great intellectual leaders.

After an account of his death, we present in this essay the more prominent themes in the articles on Ṭāhā Ḥusayn that have appeared in the Egyptian and Lebanese press, from the time of that writer's death up through December 1973.

LAST ILLNESS AND DEATH

During the last fifteen years of his life, Ṭāhā Ḥusayn had been ailing and was under the constant care of his doctor. Although largely confined to the house which he himself had built and named "Ramatān", he did, however, travel to Europe during summers. This past September 1973 he had been in Italy and returned to Egypt by sea, but on that voyage suffered from severe sea-sickness during a violent storm.

On his return his health rapidly worsened, and he died of heart failure on Sunday, October 28,1973. At his side was his French born wife of 56 years, Suzanne, to whom, he once said, he owed his love of reading. "Love of books and reading did not come to me easily - only through my wife... She it was who made reading easy for me in both French and Arabic and translations from other languages into those two. My wife is more precious to me than any book with the exception of the Qur'ān and the Gospel." (AH 29/10 p.8 ; see also p.1 and YOM 29/10 p.8).

Only the day before he died, Ṭāhā Ḥusayn was told that he had been one of six outstanding people the world over selected to receive a United Nations award (to have been bestowed on December 1, 1973) "in recognition of his work in the field of human rights, in recognition of his services to his country in the field of education, and for his outstanding leadership in the field of contemporary Arab literature." The dying man received this news with a smile. (Kamāl Mallākh[3], AH 28/10 p.8 ; 29/10 p.8).

It is said, too, that he died smiling "perhaps in joy over his country (waṭn) because he left it victorious over despair, fear, and irresolution... over his native land (bilād) which walks proud of itself, cherishing what it has of its own". (ᶜAlī ᶜAbd al-Rāziq[4], AH 31/10 p.5 ; see also Mallākh, AH 29/10 p.8).

His funeral, on Wednesday, October 31, was the first to take place on the campus of Cairo University, the same University which had granted him in 1914 its first doctorate degree. The faculty of the University, in full academic dress, accompanied the cortege to the grave, a special mausoleum to be built by the government. It will be built, with its own garden, in the al-Basatīn section of Cairo. (Mallākh, AH 30/10 p.8 ; 31/10 p.8). Hundreds of people lined the streets to bid farewell to the first Egyptian "who proclaimed that learning, like water and air, should be available for all."

Already, places have been named for him. The governor of Gizah has decreed that Ḥilmīyah al-Ahrām Street, on which Ṭāhā Ḥusayn's house stands, will henceforth bear his name. Wilcox Street in Cairo will now become Ṭāhā Ḥusayn Street by a decree of the Muḥāfiz of Cairo. The large amphitheatre (Hall Nº 74) in Cairo University, where Ṭāhā Ḥusayn lectured for nearly a quarter of a century, will now carry his name. A postage stamp, bearing an image of the writer in his later years, has just been issued. Various Egyptian and Arab cultural groups are arranging a linguistic conference in his honor, to be held on the 40th day of mourning. (Mallākh, AH 1/11 p.8). One such conference has already been held in Beirut. (MUH 2/12 p.7).

THREE THEMES

I. LIBERATION

In the newspaper articles and periodical literature examined, three distinct themes appear in the discussion of the personality and works of Ṭāhā Ḥusayn: liberation, revolution, and unification.

For many, the measure of his greatness and his immortality lies not so much in the legacy which he left as a writer, but in the fact of his personal struggle and victory over the handicap of blindness, and the circumstances of his life, its poverty and ignorance. In this sense, then, he is identified with Egypt and that with a personal life history which corresponds to the modern phase of Egypt's history, its own conscious struggle against the theme so prevalent in modern social writing in Egypt, especially since the Revolution of 1952 : the "trinity" of poverty, ignorance, and disease.

Moreover, most writers, in these articles under analysis, attribute a decisive role to Ṭāhā Ḥusayn, in the victories won thus far over ignorance, by his work for education. Thus, Yūsuf Idrīs[5] can call his death "the end of an era... which began with the onset of the dawn of Arab thought and ended with the full gleam of early morning light..." (AH 2/11 p.4).

It is the liberation he himself realized from own personal poverty and ignorance and the handicap of his blindness that has made so strong an impression on writers. In this sense Lūwīs ᶜAwaḍ declares, "Any statement about Ṭāhā Ḥusayn must begin with his most famous book, <u>al-Ayām</u>." (AH 23/11 p.4). <u>al-Yom</u> calls it "a record expressing his life: his childhood, his struggle against handicap, illness, and the misery of his situation." (YOM 29/10 p.8) "It is a study of the social structure and the cultural bases from the point of view of personal experience and is thus a sharp criticism of this structure and basis," reports Dr. Khālidah al-Sa'īd[7] (in an interview, MUH 4/11 p.7).

This personal struggle for liberation is identified, by these articles, with Egypt's own struggle in two ways. Some see Ṭāhā Ḥusayn identifying himself with Egypt's struggle and playing an active part in its liberation, as a man"... who held within his breast the aspirations of a national people (<u>Ummah</u>). Under his special guardianship and that of the <u>Ummah</u>, he led it to the light, to this century." (Yūsuf Idrīs, AH 2/11 p.4). Others express this the other way round and identify Egypt's aspirations with the life pattern of Ṭāhā Ḥusayn. "In this present phase of thought, the sons of the Arab <u>Ummah</u>," writes Dr. Zakī Najīb Maḥmūd, "are all bound by one desired goal... to combine the glories of our heritage with the new humanistic creation. This desired goal was incarnated in the person of Ṭāhā Ḥusayn in such a way that he can be considered a real model for what is necessary to achieve in this combination of the old and the new". (AH 30/10 p.5).

It has been noted above that some writers see a certain symbolism in the time of Ṭāhā Ḥusayn's death, coming just at the conclusion of the October war which represented a victory for Egypt at least over itself. Salāḥ ᶜAbd al-Subbūr[8] writes of the two "miracles", one being "the bursting forth of the Egyptian fighter," his liberation from slavish submission, from the trinity of poverty, disease, and ignorance, his discovery of fire and steel." The second miracle is that of Ṭāhā Ḥusayn "who heard in the depth of his soul the command and call of Egypt ; he set out to overcome his handicap, to rule his own destiny... who would have thought that this poor sickly youth in a threadbare galibiyah would turn out to be Ṭāhā Ḥusayn ? This is the miracle of Egypt. (AH 2/11 p.4).

Some speak of this liberation as a struggle (mukāfaḥah) against odds or as a "wrestling with fate in the affliction which stuck him in childhood". (Ḥusayn Fawzī[9], AH 2/11 p.4). "He carved out his own personality, breaking out of the circle of poverty, the gloom of ignorance in our rural areas, into the light of thought".(Mallākh, AH 29/10 p.8). Others, however, speak of it as a "revolt". Lūwīs ᶜAwaḍ reviews Ṭāhā Ḥusayn's first formative period, his years at al-Azhar (1902-10) where he was introduced to the classical Arabic literature. Here there "appeared the beginning of that intellectual revolt and spiritual agony (qalaq), that artistic and literary revolution". (AH 2/11 p.5).

Perhaps it is not at all unusual to find a Lebanese drawing attention, in this connection, to the importance of the individual. Dr. Khālidah al-Saᶜīd remarks apropos of Ṭāhā Ḥusayn's autobiography, "the individual is an important factor in development; he is capable of building himself up in spite of the obstacles of his environment. We find this principle expressed in his story, Duᶜā'al-Kirwān, wherein is apparent the secret of his own life: recourse to the intellect, will power, and the suppression of passion". (MUH 4/11 p.7). Saᶜīd al-Bustānī[10] points out that the "bitter experiences of his life", the fierce opposition he aroused, were met with "courage and a combative spirit". (MUH 2/12 p.7).

II. REVOLUTION

Ṭāhā Ḥusayn was vacationing in Italy when the July 1952 revolution took place in Egypt. He wrote to Tawfīq al-Ḥakīm on August 2, "It seems to me that literature has its rights (ḥaqq) in this glorious revolution". ("Letters from Ṭāhā Ḥusayn to Tawfiq al-Ḥakīm", AH 16/11 p.5). Although the articles under study seldom refer to Ṭāhā Ḥusayn's attitude towards the revolution of 1952, which in principle he favored, they place great emphasis on the fact that his life and work were indeed a significant revolution for Egypt.

al-Muḥarrir says his name is associated with the personality of a revolutionary writer revolting against mental stupidity (4/11 p.7). Suhayr al-Qalamāwī[11] refers to his "continuous, intellectual revolutions, revolutions against the shirking of responsiblility, against class, against confessionalism, revolutions against the cobwebs of ignorance and the thick veil of ignorance that has enveloped the people of Egypt". (AH 2/11 p.4).

But it is Lūwīs ᶜAwaḍ who analyzes these "revolutions" in detail in his full page article on Ṭāhā Ḥusayn's intellectual and social development. (AH 2/11 p.5). His clash with the Azharists led him to "break with that institution and seek new learning, new programs, new values" in the new Egyptian university.

During the second period of his intellectual formation (1910-1920) in France, "principles began to form in his consciousness, the skeleton outline of a revolutionary content, both intellectual and social." These principles he had derived from his study of Greek literature, his discovery of the unity of civilizations and the unity of man. He had also deepened his faith in intellect, freedom, and the rights of man, values he had learned, but only superficially, from Muḥammad ᶜAbduh, Qāsim Amīn, and Luṭfī al-Sayyid. The latter, together with ᶜAlī and Muṣṭafa ᶜAbd al-Rāziq, represented the "revolutionism of the elite", Dr. ᶜAwaḍ states, and this was a revolutionism of culture before it was a political one.

It was this revolutionism that Ṭāhā Husayn adhered to in the third phase of his life (1920-1930). He did not concern himself with the liberation of the masses at this time, but rather conceived his mission as leader of the cultured Egyptians and Arabs in intellectual matters, in freedom of thought, "in building up a leadership, broadly and solidly educated, which could lead Egypt and form public opinion".

Not until the fourth period (1930-1940), Dr. ᶜAwaḍ continues, do we find Ṭāhā Ḥusayn defending the freedom of the masses. "From being a symbol of the cultured, his image changes to become the symbol of the people... the masses were indeed victorious in the intense struggle for the return of the 1923 Constitution and the return of Ṭāhā Ḥusayn to the university in 1935".

Dr. ᶜAwaḍ goes on to describe Ṭāhā Ḥusayn's work in the Ministry of Education as more effective than his writing, "as is shown in every school, university, and institute he opened, in every student to whom he granted the opportunity for opening his mind to learning." (AH 2/11 p.5). Others also refer to his work in education as revolutionary. <u>al-Muḥarrir</u> considers his establishing free education for all as "the first revolution in education in the Arab world." (MUH 4/11 7 ; see also Muḥammad Anīs, AH 2/11 p.4 and Suhayr al-Qalamāwī, <u>ibid</u>.)

Ṭāhā Ḥusayn's work on pre-Islamic poetry is singled out for special emphasis ; " revolution in contemporary Arab thought and its liberation from the chains of the past", writes <u>al-Yom</u> (29/10 p.8), "our first intellectual revolution", declares <u>al-Balāgh</u> (12/11 pp. 33, 34), emphasizing that its intellectual aspect was much more important than the religious, although it was the latter that first drew attention because of the criticism from certain religious traditionalists.

Dr. ᶜAwaḍ also emphasizes this point, calling the "scientific method", which Ṭāhā Ḥusayn applied in his study on pre-Islamic poetry, "a major revolution of the 20's". In an allusion to the philosophy of Descartes and of positivism which greatly influenced Ṭāhā Ḥusayn, Dr. ᶜAwaḍ states "no longer would the logic of 'I hear, therefore I am' suffice, but rather, "I think, therefore I am'". Hence, he concludes, the important thing that Ṭāhā Husayn put forth in the '20's is that the proof from tradition is not enough, that traditions of the ancients or the moderns are not enough, but everything must be subjected to an intellectual demonstration through inductive reasoning. In this sense, Ṭāhā Ḥusayn opened the door of ijtihād (personal effort) in literary, intellectual, and historical research after this door had been locked for one thousand years, since the Arab dawlah (empire) in the classical period." (AH 2/11 p.5).

III. UNIFICATION

Even more prominent than the themes of liberation and revolution in these several articles under study is the theme of unification, and this despite the fact -- or perhaps because of it -- that Ṭāhā Ḥusayn experienced within himself a painful division. His physical blindness is constantly contrasted with the brilliance of his mind. (See, e.g. Mallākh, AH 29/10 p.8). Lūwīs ᶜAwaḍ referring to Ṭāhā Ḥusayn's early career speaks of his being, at one and the same time, in harmony and at odds with himself, in harmony at being an educated intellectual in the same class with the elite, but at odds with himself because of his inborn attraction to the masses. (AH 2/11 p.5). Even though one of his main efforts was to show how Egypt belonged to the European tradition and civilization, Ṭāhā Ḥusayn bears witness to the painful division he felt within himself, when he wrote to Tawfīq al-Ḥakīm on Aug. 3, 1952, "my corpse is here in Italy, but my soul in Egypt, and between the two there is a broad land and a wide sea". Only two years later he expressed an attraction pulling him in the opposite direction. "At present, I am most abstemious of all in (Arabic) literature, most weary of it, fed up with it .. and like nothing more than to read, and that in foreign literature, French, Italian American..." ("Letters...", AH 16/11 p.5).

Some of the articles place great emphasis on the power Ṭāhā Ḥusayn had to unify the various aspects of culture. Three of the four lessons which Lūwīs ᶜAwaḍ says Ṭāhā Ḥusayn taught us concern this unification: that there is no dividing line between culture (thaqāfah) and society, between literature and life; that the old has no freshness and vigor except in the new; that there is no nationalism (qawmīyah) without humanism and no humanism without nationalism. (AH 29/10 p.5).

In a later article ᶜAwaḍ stresses the work Ṭāhā Ḥusayn did to bring

> "the educated out of their political isolation and to smash the massive obstacle which separated thought from life, culture from society, the elite from the masses... Hence the separation Ṭāhā Ḥusayn made from the party of nobles and the powerful... and his adherence to the party of the struggling masses for the sake of their freedom and their rights has a special significance in the history of modern Egypt: abolished was the gap between thought and life, the obstacle between intellect and emotion." (AH 2/11 p.5; see also Suhayr Qalamāwī, AH 2/11 p.4).

Dr. Zakī Maḥmūd puts much stress on Ṭāhā Ḥusayn's ability to take the best from the past heritage, to became intimate with the great figures of the past, writing of them "as if in conversation with them... not as a blind follower, perplexed, confused like one wandering among statues carved out of stones... but as one of them and in converse with them. Thus he took from the past material from which he shaped a present and a future". (AH 30/10 p.5 ; see also ᶜAlī ᶜAbd al-Rāziq, AH 31/10 p.5 ; NAH 3/11 p.5).

Yūsuf al-Khāl[12] sees the importance Ṭāhā Ḥusayn gave to the intellect as the basic reason why he could so successfully link the past with the present for "the past does not become the present or the future except on a foudation, and that fondation is the intellect, which grows from birth and is nourished by education". Commenting on Ṭāhā Ḥusayn's important work, <u>The Future of Culture in Egypt</u>, Yūsuf al-Khāl develops the concept of the civilizing role Egypt had played in its past history, a role that "must return to her, a return that will come through a pursuit of the ancient and modern heritage..." (NAH SUP 4/11 p.3).

The articles surveyed also remark on the cultural unification Ṭāhā Ḥusayn believed existed between Europe and Egypt. Ḥusayn Fawzī goes so far as to say, concerning the work, <u>The Future of Culture in Egypt</u>, that it is "the standard by which is measured our progress or regression in the domain of culture and civilization." He draws attention to the University of Alexandria, which Ṭāhā Ḥusayn founded to be a "bridge between Egypt and Europe". (AH 2/11 p.4).

Dr. Zāhiyah al-Qaddūrah[13] and others also refer to Ṭāhā Ḥusayn's theory of cultural unification, but on a more universal scale. "He was one of those who believed in the continuity of cultures and the conjunction between world civilization and Arab-Islamic civilization", Dr. al-Qaddūrah states. (MUH 4/11 p.7 ; see also NAH SUP 4/11 pp. 3,4; Ṣubhi Ṣalih[14] in MUH 2/12 p.7).

The writers who draw attention to the fact that the identification with European civilization is being rejected today in Egyptian and Arab circles, nevertheless describe this identification as justified in the circumstances of Egypt in the 30's as a necessary reaction by an educated person like Ṭāhā Ḥusayn against the backwardness of Egypt, particularly in science, liberty, respect for the individual and justice. (See Khālidah al-Saᶜīd, MUH 4/11 p.7 and Unsī al-Hajj[15], NAH SUP 4/11 p.15).

Nearly all the articles refer to Ṭāhā Ḥusayn's famous dictum that education for all should be as free as water and air. They see in this principle, to achieve which Ṭāhā Ḥusayn's devoted his years in the Ministry of Education, a force which does away with the barrier between culture and the masses. (See e.g. Muḥammad Anīs, AH 2/11 p. 4; Lūwīs ᶜAwaḍ, AH 2/11 p. 5; AH 31/10 p. 5). Lūwīs ᶜAwad points to Ṭāhā Ḥusayn's "second period of formation" (1910-1920) as the time when he discovered the "unity of man by reason of the unity of advanced civilizations and values". (AH 2/11 p. 5)

One interesting exception to this theme of unification occurs, and this in the realm of religion. In marked contrast to his efforts to unify culture and the masses, intellect and emotion, different world cultures, nationalism and humanism, the old and the new .. Ṭāhā Husayn is described as a strong proponent of the separation of religion from the state, an advocate of nation-building on the secular idea of the state. (MUH 4/11 p.7).
Yūsuf al-Khāl points out that he called for secular education with-

out religion "except in the role of a spring which slakes the soul athirst for it", and maintained that in politics, religion, despite its importance, "should not prevail over the direction of political life". (NAH SUP 4/11 p.3). Ghālī Shukrī[16] concerns himself with defending Ṭāhā Ḥusayn from the charge of apostasy or atheism or for being a "materialist" thinker. Because he was able to separate the intellectual from the domination of traditional religious concepts is no indication that Ṭāhā Ḥusayn "was a non-believer or an apostate.(BAL 12/11 p.34).

CONCLUSION

These, then, are the principal themes which stand out in the articles written about Ṭāhā Ḥusayn after his death. Perhaps another point should be noted in conclusion. It is not so much a theme as a tone which underlines nearly all these articles, and that is their optimism. Ṭāhā Ḥusayn, as was noted above, died with a smile on his face. Kamāl Mallākh sees this as symbolizing the character and personality of the man (AH 29/10 p.8; also 31/10 p.5), and Dr. Zakī Najīb Maḥmūd points out that "he was a luminary for our age, a humanist... he believed in progress, he was optimistic for the future." (AH 30/10 p.5). Ṭāhā Ḥusayn, says Bint al-Shāṭi'[17], "was a light to us on the road of our existence... one who gave our entire existence a value, a meaning, and a vision". (AH 31/10 p.5) His death, in fact, evokes not so much sentiments of grief and loss, but rather those of hope for the future of Egypt, because, like Ṭāhā Ḥusayn, Egypt has struggled and has come out victorious over the despair of poverty, ignorance and disease. His death came just as that despair was departing from the soul of Egypt, as Tawfīq al-Ḥakīm stated in his eulogy.

Perhaps it was this basic optimism towards the world -- and the Arab world in particular, that made Ṭāhā Ḥusayn so open to the west and non-Arab cultures. A pessimistic outlook seems invariably to narrow the scope of one's outlook. Considerable self-confidence and a certain optimism have already become evident in Egyptian society since the October war, as the articles on Ṭāhā Ḥusayn demonstrate. This confidence in themselves creates an atmosphere that will enable the Arabs to confront more easily the continuing challenge of western culture and values. Many writers in the media have recently pointed out that the October war will initiate a new era in Arabic literature and arts, quite different in tone from the pessimism, despair, and lack of purpose that characterized Arab letters after the June war of 1967. (18)

Nevertheless, the conflicts between modernization and the older traditions have not been resolved by the October war, however confident and optimistic its outcome may have left writers and intellectuals. Moreover, Ṭāhā Husayn's leadership belonged to the earlier liberal phase in Egyptian culture and letters and not to the more recent period of the Nasserite Revolution when Arab nationalism, Arab socialism and the reaction against more subtle forms of imperialism served to cast doubt on European culture as a model to be adopted by modern Egypt and the Arab world, as Ṭāhā Ḥusayn had proposed. His task in bringing Egypt into the modern world on a western pattern was as Yūsuf al-

Khāl remarks, "accomplished before the cancer of Israel stretched out over the Arab world and usurped all concerns." (NAH SUP 4/11 p.3)

Some like Yūsuf al-Khāl, will continue to harken back to the active years of Ṭāhā Ḥusayn and call upon the Arabs to follow his leadership by asserting, "we must become Europeans in everything..." (ibid. p.4) Others, however, -- doubtless the majority -- will reflect the conflict evident in Ṭāhā Ḥusayn's own life and works ("my corpse is here in Italy, but my soul in Egypt") -- the pull in several cultural directions at once which is Egypt's dilemma. Dr. Ḥusayn Fawzī has well expressed it. He commented on Ṭāhā Ḥusayn's concern, cited earlier, that the University of Alexandria be the bridge between Egypt and Europe, and he recalled Alexandria's unique position as the city "which places Egypt in the stream of civilization existing to the north of the Mediterranean Sea. "Dr. Fawzī then adds," just as the Nile is the link between Egypt and Central Africa, the Sinai Peninsula the solid bond with the Arab-East, and the Red Sea our road to the civilization of Asia". (AH 2/11 p.4) Egypt must still continue the search for its identity along these several paths yet remain somehow independent of each.

NOTES

1. Egyptian philosopher, professor, journalist, editor of al-Adīb (Kuwait), author of The Renewal of Arab Thought, editor of now defunct journals, al-Thaqāfah and al-Fikr al-Maᶜāsir.

2. Egyptian writer concerned with the problem of cultural identity.

3. Egyptian artist, archeologist, author, born 1918. Has been illustrator and art critic for al-Ahrām and Akhbār al-Yawm. Now writes regular column in al-Ahrām, "Min ghayr ᶜAnwān" (Without title).

4. Egyptian, Director of Education.

5. Prominent Egyptian fiction writer and playwrit, born 1927. Emphasizes social themes. Expelled from Arab Socialist Union in February 1973, then reinstated. (See recent interview with him in Beirut, MUH 21/12 p.8)

6. Egyptian literary critic for al-Ahrām, leftist. He was dismissed from the Arab Socialist Union in February, 1973, then reinstated. (See CEMAM Reports I, 1. p. 74)

7. Lebanese literary critic. Her doctorate thesis at the Sorbonne, Paris, was entitled, Renewal in Contemporary Arabic Literature after World War II.

8. Prominent Egyptian poet and poetic dramatist.

9. Egyptian writer and intellectual, born 1900. Under-Secretary of State in the Ministry of Culture and National Guidance (1955-1960). Author of Sindabad al-Miṣri, an effort to rediscover the Egyptian personality.

10. Lebanese intellectual, educator, born 1921, professor at Lebanese University and St. Joseph University. At one time Director of Schools and Inspector for Ministry of Education.

11. Egyptian writer and translator of English literature, doctor in literature from the University of Cairo.

12. Lebanese Christian poet and writer, co-founder with the poet Adonīs, of the periodical of modern Arabic poetry, al-Shi^{c}r.

13. Lebanese, dean of the faculty of Liberal Arts at the Lebanese University.

14. Lebanese Muslim Shaykh, co-author with Père Y. Moubarac of "Le dialogue islamo-chrétien au Liban," in Conférences du Cénacle, Beirut Nº. 19 (1965) pp. 17-72.

15. Lebanese journalist, author, poet, born 1937, editor-in-chief of al-Nahār's weekly supplement.

16. Egyptian, residing in Lebanon, literary critic, writes on contemporary Arab fiction.

17. Pseudo-name for ^{c}Ā 'ishah ^{c}Abd al-Raḥmān, Egyptian; writes on social problems from the woman's point of view, also on Islam.

18. See, e.g., series of articles on "Post October War Arabic Literature"; first, of series. (MUH 28/11 p.7)

SIX DOCUMENTS ON MUSLIM "PARTICIPATION" IN THE NATIONAL LIFE OF LEBANON

by the CEMAM Staff

The delicate religious or "confessional" equilibrium which characterizes Lebanon is easily threatened by any crisis which seems to call for firm, decisive action. May 1973 was such a crisis. The confrontation between the Lebanese Army and the Palestine Resistance put to the test that equilibrium. The Beirut papers published some documents and interpretations of events which are useful for understanding the attitudes of the Muslim communities. We present here six of these documents. But first it is necessary to present briefly the situation which threatened the confessional balance.

On April 10 Israeli commandoes assassinated three Palestinian leaders in Beirut. This provoked the resignation of the Salam government on April 13. Beginning April 18 Amin al-Hafiz set about forming a cabinet. Traditional political leaders, especially the Sunnites, judged his choice of ministers as too weak and not sufficiently representative.

Meanwhile, incidents with the Palestinians increased. al-Hafiz had not yet received the approbation of the Chamber (he never did) when on May 2 the incidents with the Palestinians led to a confrontation of the Army with the Resistance. Delegates from Arab countries filed into Beirut as mediators and, finally, on May 7 an accord was reached between the Army and the Resistance. However, a few hours later the confrontation recommenced more violently than before. al-Hafiz proclaimed a state of emergency, then presented his resignation on May 8. At the same time Syria closed its borders with Lebanon.

From that moment, and for an extended period, the President (Maronite) and the Army (whose chief is also Maronite) were the sole official authorities responsible for the decisions which had to be taken in the very delicate situation which had put Lebanon in confrontation with the Palestinian Resistance and Syria, and, in a sense, with the other Arab states. The negotiations which followed brought to the fore the leader of al-Sa'iqa (a Palestinian Resistance group subordinate to the Syrian Ba'th) and terminated in an accord on May 17. On May 23 the state of emergency was lifted.

al-Hafiz withdrew his resignation on May 19, but could not form a government which would be acceptable to the Chamber. His successor, Takieddin Solh, appointed on June 21, did not succeed in forming a cabinet till July 8. On August 17, Syria opened the borders.

During that long period of national tension - four months - the unity of the country was never really threatened. 1973 was very different from 1958. Not only was there no armed confrontation betwenn Lebanese communities, but the religious leaders of the communities by their frequent meetings among themselves and with diverse authorities consciously set about demonstrating and guaranteeing unity. Finally, the resolution of tensions showed itself in a call for renewed "participation".

The Mufti of the Sunnites had been the first of the religious leaders to go to the President (May 8). This was quite natural given the absence of a Sunnite Prime Minister. But the Mufti later remained in the wings, as did the Maronite religious leaders. The other community leaders were more manifest. The Shiite Imam was especially active, offering himself as intermediary with Syria (whose President is an Alawite) and animating the meetings of religious leaders.

The role of the Shiite Imam is complex : he felt responsibility for South Lebanon evacuated by the army for the confrontation in the capital and in the Baqqā^{c}, and he has been active in trying to raise the economic and social level of his community which is as numerous as, but less influential than, the Maronite and Sunnite communities. At the same time, he was clearly taking a position contrary to a faction of the Shiite community which has its spokesman in the President of the Chamber and which appeared to be basically in accord with the President of the Republic. In short, in the abnormal political void, religious leaders and religio-political organizations came forth to express the discontent and desires of their communities.

Sunnites and Shiites demanded "participation", but for the Sunnites the demands were more political, whereas those of the Shiites were more social. The explanation is clear. The presence of Sunnites at the top echelon of the government and in the machinery of the State as co-responsibles by right assures the community an eminent place in the country and assures Lebanon a certain solidarity with the other Arab countries which are predominantly Muslim.

The presence of the Palestinians is a continual reminder of that latter role. Accordingly, the Sunnites oppose a shift towards a presidential regime. Some make an occasional call for "deconfessionalization" of state functions but in terms which mean their own fuller participation. For the Shiite community, poor and exposed to Israeli incursions in the South, participation means a fairer share of government directorates and a more just distribution of goods in a country growing relatively rich.

Sunnite demands for participation were in part fulfilled by the formation of the Solh government. Shiite demands remain an issue.

The following translations present rather clearly one fix on the kaleidescope of Lebanese community politics, set by the events of May. The six documents are as follows:

1. The National Pact of Islamic Organizations, 1955.

2. The Maqāsid Graduates Statement on the Lebanese-Palestinian Crisis, May, 1973.

3. "The lesson of Recent Events", Statement by Amīn al-Araisi, President of al-Hay'āt al-Wataniyya (National Organizations) and President of the Executive Committee for Islamic Organizations and Associations, June, 1973.

4. The Shiite "Pact" of June 22, 1973.

5. Letter of Imam Musa Sadr to the Members of the Supreme Islamic Shiite Council, December 1973.

6. Memorandum to Prime Minister Takieddin Solh on Shiite Demands, July 1973.

1. THE NATIONAL PACT OF ISLAMIC ORGANIZATIONS, 1955.

INTRODUCTION:

One basic document for an understanding of the current situation of Muslims in Lebanon is the National Pact of Muslim Organizations, signed in 1955 by the presidents of six Muslim organizations. The five articles of this document set forth ways of removing governmental prejudice against Muslims, especially in public life.

This statement is to be distinguished from the National Pact, an unwritten agreement worked out in 1943, largely by the first President of Lebanon, the Maronite Bishara al-Khuri, and the first Prime Minister, Riyad al-Solh. This 1943 agreement embodies what has been called constructive confessionalism, i.e., the seats in parliament and other government positions are to be distributed among the various sects in Lebanon in proportion to their numbers in the population.[1] Muslims have generally appealed to the National Pact when they have felt deprived of a fair participation in government positions.

TEXT:[+]

Whereas the stability of the government in Lebanon cannot be realized except by genuine cooperation between the two groups of citizens, Muslims and Christians, of whom the Lebanese Republic is composed, and whereas that cooperation cannot be accomplished except by the distribution of rights among associates on the basis of justice, fairness and equity, and whereas the Muslims in Lebanon are equal in numbers, with the slightest modification, to their Christian brothers, while in the present distribution of functions and institutions in the state there is a clear prejudice against the rights of the Muslims, and whereas justice, on the one hand, and desire for national unity, on the other hand, oblige the elements of the country to cooperate to remove this prejudice, and whereas article 95 of the Constitution guarantees the principle of justice and the spirit of concord among the citizens, for the sake of this sincere cooperation the undersigned have drawn up this pact and have committed themselves to work for its realization by all legal means.

+ from al-Hayat, 31 May 1973, pp. 1, 8.

1 See M. W. Suleiman, Political Parties in Lebanon (Ithaca, N.Y.; 1967) pp. 21-23.

Article one. Let benefits and institutions and functions in the government and in all the agencies of public service be distributed on the basis of equality among Muslims and Christians, and let there be taken into consideration in this distribution both type and number of the functionaries, so that the Muslims will receive their just, legal share of the ministerial portfolios and chief directorates and of representation abroad and all posts, especially those that are directive (tawjīhīyah).

Article two. Let the seats of the Chamber of Deputies, whatever their number, be distributed equally among Muslims and Christians until there is a new census.

Article three. The signers of this pact engage themselves to support the men of the government and any other citizens who hold high office as long as they remain desirous of respecting this pact and of working for its execution. The signers will also withdraw their confidence from, and announce their opposition to, all who contravene it.

Article four. The representatives of the Muslims in the Ministries and in the Chamber engage themselves to abide by this pact and to work for its realization; and the Prime Minister engages himself in a special way to place these demands in the forefront of the conditions on which his acceptance of power is based. Also the candidates for this post will obligate themselves not to accept power except on this basis. What is applicable to the Prime Minister is applicable to every Muslim Minister in the government. However, in case the Prime Minister resigns from his post in despair of realizing the articles of this pact, the candidates for this post will undertake that no one of them will accept to take over the office except on condition that the causes for which the former Prime Minister withdrew from power be removed and that the demands of the Muslims be met.

Article five. If the irregular situation continues, depriving Muslims of their legal rights to functions and institutions, and if the responsible people do not hasten to correct the situation by fulfilling Muslim demands, then the Muslims will consider that there is on the part of the President an aversion to applying the regulations of the Constitution and a withdrawal from his repeated promises of fairness towards the Muslims. In this case the signers of this pact will be bound to take all the means and measures which will guarantee the attainment of their legal constitutional rights.

President of the Islamic Council, Husayn al-Owaini

President of the Social Cell, Abdallah al-Mashnūq

President of the National Organization, Dr. Muhammad Khalid

President of the League of Beirut Families, Dr. Nasīb al-Barbīr

President of the Federation of Islamic Youth, Dr. Muhammad Knaio

President of the Najjāda Party, Adnan Hakīm

2. THE MAQASID GRADUATES STATEMENT ON THE LEBANESE-PALESTINIAN CRISIS, MAY, 1973.

INTRODUCTION :

As a result of the government crisis in Lebanon provoked by the Israeli attack on Beirut in April 1973, and the Lebanese Army-Palestinian confrontation in early May, various Muslim groups registered protests against the state of emergency which had been declared and which left them bereft of effective power and participation in the government. One of the demands for participation came from the graduates of the Maqāsid.

The significance of the Maqāsid's declaration may be suggested by its make-up and its history. The "Maqāsid" (sometimes spelled Makassid in European languages) is the term generally used for the organization known as the Muslim Benevolent Society for the Education of Muslim Youth. Established late in the 19th century through the private initiative of members of the Sunni Muslim community, the society laid the foundation for a Muslim educational revival in Lebanon. Although hostile to the Western institutions established in Lebanon, the Maqāsid attempted to combine the principles of Islam with modern western ideas in order to give an education suited to modern needs. This society has played a significant role in developing a modern and upwardly mobile Sunni middle class through the graduates of its schools. Some of the most important Muslim families are connected with it, and Sā'ib Salām, former Prime Minister, has served as its president.

In view of this success, it is not surprising that the Maqāsid and its members have become aware of the significant role they can play in Lebanese politics, representing, as they see it, the Sunni community in defence of its rights, especially the right of participation in the government of Lebanon.

On May 19, 1973, two days after the cease fire was arranged between the Lebanese Army and the Palestinian Resistance, and on the day on which the Prime Minister Amīn al-Hafiz withdrew his resignation, while the state of emergency was still in force (it was lifted for Beirut on May 23), a meeting of Islamic associations and personalities was held at the Maqāsid headquarters.[1] Dr. ᶜIzzat Ḥarb, President of

1) In an earlier statement the Maqāsid had criticized Pres. Franjieh for saying that "the presence of an occupying army (i.e. the Palestinian Resistance) is something no Lebanese can accept", and accused him a) of going against the constitutional demand for democratic participation in the government; and b) of having trained guns on the West Quarter of Beirut where thousands of Muslims live; this is the first time since 1958 that this has happened. (YOM 5/5/73 p. 3)

the Maqāsid, read a statement which those present all agreed to. Thus, although the document is described as having been issued by the Maqāsid Graduates, it is also used by all the other groups. (N 21/5 p. 3)

After the reading of the document, several members proceeded to comment on it. The Prime Minister at the time, Dr. Amin al-Hafiz, "welcomed the document, even though he did not embrace everything it contained with regard to strengthening the position of the Prime Minister".

In the discussion, various members:

1) stated that the common danger all Lebanese must face is Israel, and the continuation of the state of emergency with its violation of democratic tradition prevents the confrontation of this common enemy;

2) criticized those who have ignored the rights of Muslims;

3) called for a democratic constitution by the abolition of confessionalism and the institution of secularization in all government positions;

4) cited historical examples where the National Pact of 1943 did not, in fact, distribute the principal responsibilities on a confessional basis; and

5) called for the formation of a committee which would present the demands of the present meeting to the President of the Republic. These demands were;

   a) the cessation of the state of emergency;

   b) the formation without delay of a national (watanīya) government, and

   c) the support of the Palestinian Resistance.

TEXT:+

In our efforts for Lebanon and our desire for her democracy; in our belief in responsible freedom; for the sake of an effective national unity based on the representation of the will of all the citizens, and, consequently, on their sense of belonging to the country with equality as citizens; in order that the blood of combatants may not be spilled and innocent people not die in vain and thus repeat the mindless tragedies and crisis of the past; in the conviction of those ideals which have inspired and continue to inspire the citizens and those of their sons who have struggled for this country since it embarked on the road to independence before 1943; in order that Lebanon may remain always as its free citizens wish it to remain: a country of mutual understanding shared among all, and of productive

+from Sawt al-Sha^{c}b, 25 May 1973, p. 3.

cooperation among all its sons, a part of the Arab nation, a nation which is struggling for its freedom and unity, a center for the diffusion of ideas which is committed to the national Arab cause, a fatherland for those sacred freedoms which lay down the fundamental condition by which every country comes to birth, a country governed through the national pact which was established on the sharing of responsibilities among the citizens according to justice and equality;

WE UNDERSTAND, that during ordeals peace is not possible for this country, nor security for its development, nor is there present the basis for national and democratic dialogue among the people except through absolute loyalty to principles, the infrigement of which has created in the past and still creates in the present a situation of national deviation which has always been at the root of Lebanon's constant crisis and disturbances.

1. Presidency of the Government

The Lebanese Constitution, despite its being somewhat out of date, has established the democratic parliamentary regime. The fundamental principles of this form of government are well known by everyone. One of these principles is that the head of the government chooses the government after being authorized to do so. The government alone carries out the mandate of governing and alone bears the consequences of governing, nor does it share this governing with any other. The decisions of the Ministerial Council of Ministers are passed by majority vote without the vote of the President of Republic, the government not being responsible to the President of the Republic. The government is responsible to the Parliament which embodies the popular and sovereign will.

The President of Republic cannot sign any decree without the approval (muwāfaqah) of the duly qualified minister and the approval of the Head of the Government, the Minister being the head of his ministry and the decision maker in carrying out its tasks. The President of the republic should be an arbiter, not a faction or party. The principle of non-responsibility of the Head of State imposes on him the obligation of not making public utterance on any opinion, declaration or official statement.

We make the observation that what is taking place among us now is against all constitutional usages and principles. The President of the Republic is practicing the full power possessed by the French High Commissioner during the time of the mandate. He is thus arrogating to himself all authority; he is forming both the interior and exterior policy of Lebanon and conducting himself as if he were the head of government.

This kind of activity halts the operation of democracy within the prescriptions specified by the constitution and enjoined by the national pact and has led to a constitutional void and the extension of the state of emergency in order to suppress liberties and to intimidate the people. It has created a state of siege against the national movement and the Palestinian Resistance and allowed only one line of thought by poisoning public opinion in the country, and by the use of force and arms through heavy weapons and aircraft in striking the Resistance and loyal citizens, a thing which never happened before, not even in the 1958 events which isolated the people for a long time from some of the politicians directly responsible for them. The people cannot forget the effect of those events. The same kind of thing is inevitable this time also.

2. National and Democratic Balance in the Institutions of the State .

The state is for all citizens. The citizens are equal in rights and duties. However, recent events have proven to us each day that there are flaws in the national and democratic equilibrium, which flaws allow for the favoring of a particular group. As a result, a realization has grown, on the part of a majority of citizens, that the state is one thing and the nation another and that the present government does not represent its country, Lebanon.

Thus we find, in the institutions of education responsible for creating a new and liberated generation of Lebanese, a domination over the positions of power, the programs, and the policies.

In the institutions for defense and security, we find that responsibility for the defense of the country, the task of repelling the enemy, and the legal prosecution of spies and saboteurs are monopolized by positions of power. These positions alone undertake defense and security planning in opposition to the national principle which declares that the defense of the national frontiers and the country's honor are duties and privileges which belong to all the citizens. But a military plan without power to engage in actual combat and the possession of defensive weapons without actual resistance to the enemy do not represent the will of all the Lebanese.

Again, a quick move was made to weaken the popular representative institutions and the vanguard of the Chamber of Deputies, to paralyze their activity, and to oppose the sincere elements within them. All of that was done so that the centers of power in the country might remain in the hands of the executive authority on which the President of the Republic keeps an eye and which he directs, contrary to the articles of the constitution.

For this reason the citizens do not have during crisis a sense of the presence of the Chamber of Deputies despite the fact that it is the source of all powers. It is the Chamber which is skilled in the task of law-making and watches over the activities of the government and guides its steps towards what is good for the country.

One of the results of this deliberate infringement of the balance of power, a balance agreed upon for the chief institutions of the government, is the accumulation of mandatory power and the concentration of powers of decision and execution in the hands of a single group. Thus we have witnessed the spectacle of the state during these critical days acting as if there were no government, and no parliament, but with the chief of state assuming an imperious attitude, and those responsible for security complying with this.

3. The Palestinian Presence

We acknowledge the Palestinian presence in Lebanon not so much as a fact, but as a national right.

The Palestinians are our brothers; their cause is our cause; their destiny is our destiny. If we look upon Palestine as a part of the greater nation, then preparation for liberation of this stolen part is a responsibility of all the Arabs. And if those living in the Palestinian Camps are foremost in supplying themselves with arms and preparing themselves for the day of liberation, then it is our duty to support them, to strengthen them, and to join their ranks.

The whole of the Arab nation is threatened with the Zionist danger. No longer is there anyone in Lebanon who denies the fact that Israel covets Lebanon's territory and its water. The Palestine revolution is an Arab revolution, and the arms which it desires to increase will never be used except against the enemy. Whatever attack is undertaken against the enemy or whatever resistance is offered to it expresses a security for Lebanon and a defense against danger to the country. The expression "army of occupation" used in reference to the armed Palestinians in Lebanon is a terminology to be rejected.

This note was not heard when the Algerian army of liberation trained for more than seven years in Tunisia and Morocco in order to liberate Algeria from French colonization. Nor was this note ever heard when there was in Britain during the Second World War more than half a million French and European soldiers training for all kinds of warfare with light and heavy weapons in preparation for liberating their homeland.

We have called on the Palestinians to engage the enemy in the occupied territories while forbidding them to draw near to its borders. We have called on them to give up the carrying of arms in our cities and their suburbs while failing to provide them with protection from enemy attacks.

And if, God forbid, the enemy should one day occupy part of Lebanon or the whole of it, and drive out some of its citizens, would it not be natural that a Lebanese army of liberation be formed in Syria or some other Arab country, and that it demand freedom of action and training in bearing arms for the purpose of liberating the homeland ?

The Lebanese are agreed in principle concerning the liberation of Palestine and their responsibility for undertaking a share in the battle of liberation. Other than this assertion in principle there is no real participation with the resistance in this responsibility. However, the value of this responsibility and this participation in the struggle for liberation is to be measured by Lebanon's pre-eminent capacity to be a developing civilized country within which are found education, science, and universities.

There is no sincerity towards Palestine while there exist false dealings with the Resistance. There is no value to written formulas and agreements except in so far as they are in agreement with the above-mentionned goal and are faithful to the common Arab interest in the task of liberation which includes the Palestinians, the Lebanese, and all the Arabs in general.

Lebanon is a small country with no protection except its adherence to principles and values. Every disdain of principles and values in the internal affairs of the country, in dealings within the Arab world, and on the international level is a serious national sin which inflicts a loss upon Lebanon, its assets, its existence, its frontiers and is a threat to its Lebanese and Arab character.

These truths are an inseparable part of the national conscience. They are standards by which all deviations, all political activity responsible for placing Lebanon on more than one occasion on the brink of national suicide, are to be judged.

The general task in Lebanon, whether concerning the responsibilities of the government or those of social, cultural, and political leadership, is bound up with fidelity to these fundamental truths which the repeated and severe crises in Lebanon serve to uncover. The consciousness of these truths can be an aid in liberating the country and the citizens and can help in establishing a national democratic existence which is internally cohesive and capable of fulfilling its Arab and international role.

What is most important about these truths is that they have become, in the growing political consciousness of this present era of Lebanon's history, a possession of all citizens in their general awareness of the problems of their country and the crisis which agitate it. No one active in the public domain can be unaware of that. It is incumbent upon all of us to be deeply aware of the results consequent to these truths and to act upon them with all sincerity and fidelity.

Beirut, 19 May 1973

President of the Organization
the lawyer, 'Izzat Harb

3. "THE LESSON OF THE RECENT EVENTS" BY THE ADVOCATE AMIN AL-ARAISI, PRESIDENT OF AL-HAYAT AL-WATANIYYA (NATIONAL ORGANIZATIONS) AND PRESIDENT OF THE EXECUTIVE COMMITTEE FOR ISLAMIC ORGANIZATIONS AND INSTITUTIONS.

INTRODUCTION:

This statement concerns the complaints of Muslims about their lack of proper participation in national life, complaints which came to a head in the demand for the resignation of Dr. Amin al-Hafiz, the Prime Minister.

TEXT:+

Now that the resignation of Dr. Amin al-Hafiz' government has been accepted, a review of the stages which led to this result is inevitable. This review is contrary to what was spread abroad and circulated by some, concerning the actual events which preceded and accompanied this resignation.

The fact is that the moves of the Islamic organizations began six months ago, in the period of President Salam's government, when on the day of the blessed Feast of Sacrifice, the Islamic organizations supported the demand of the religious leaders to reject the official government protocol.[1] Then, before the formation of the government of Dr. al-Hafiz, the demand for participation was made in a meeting held at the headquarters of al-Hay'āt al-Wataniyya. This meeting was provoked by a single handed assumption of power and the lack of respect for the Presidency of the Council of Ministers.[2] al-Hafiz was charged with forming a government, and all circles welcomed the nomination. But the new government was formed without concern for true representation, especially with regard to the portfolios.[3] This neglect led to an increase of resentment and a loss of the feeling of participation. In the wake of this came the rally of al-Hay'āt al-Wataniyya in which all the Muslim organizations and parties in Beirut and its environs participated. They all expressed their loud refusal to accept the existing situation.[4]

Then came the painful events with the victims, the shelling by cannon and the bombing by planes of quarters on the West side.[5] This was what led to uncontrollable resentment among the Muslims, especially after the serious mistake the government of al-Hafiz committed in announcing a state of emergency. The (dubious) justifications used to support the decla-

+from al-Hayat, 17 June 1973, p. 1.

ration of a state of emergency which al-Hafiz personally announced on television (only increased resentment). Then, after some hours, came the resignation of al-Hafiz. This left power in the hands of one party (<u>jiha</u>) and created a constitutional vacuum.

After all that had happened, al-Hafiz' consequent withdrawal of his resignation could never be accepted, no matter what the conditions.[6] Because his government was considered constitutionally responsible, it had of necessity to bear responsibility for the events before the people who had suffered. The government's resignation had to be the first expiation for its guilt.

Faced with this reality, the Islamic organizations were obliged to publish their historic declaration in which they demanded the resignation of the government and the boycotting of the vote of confidence.[7] The truly popular feelings from which this idea sprang enabled the Islamic organizations to consolidate their support, not only among Muslim deputies but also among their brothers from other groups who stood gratefully by their side, desirous of national unity.[8]

For these reasons we can say that the crisis which surrounded al-Hafiz did not end with his resignation.[9] It preceded it and will survive it as long as active participation in power is not made a reality by the application of the constitution in a true fashion, and as long as democracy in government is not practiced with regard to all, without any single-handed performances.

The Muslims in Lebanon are not confessional-minded, nor are they opposed to progress. No, they only desire true social justice and active participation in power.

At this crucial time we call on all Muslim men in politics to unify their ranks, and to speak with one voice in guarding the dignity and rights of those whom they represent.

<u>Notes</u> :

1 ^{c}Id al-Adha, January 14, 1973. The Lebanese government had announced on December 19, 1972 that its President would personally participate in the celebration of only a limited number of feasts, none of them religious.

As the ^{c}Id al-Adha approached, the Prime Minister Sā^{c}ib Salām decided to be out of the country (in Hungary) during the feast, thus avoiding an unpleasant confrontation with Muslims who were insisting that he fulfill the promise he had made to declare Friday an official "day off". As a result of the uproar among Muslims at this decision of the Prime Minister to be away, the government decided to have a Minister, Jamīl Kibbi, be its official representative at the ^{c}Id al-Adha. (This is the "protocol" referred to in Amīn al-Araisi's statement).

When Muslims declared that they would receive the Minister only if he renewed the Prime Minister's promise about the Friday holiday, the government revoked its decision to send a representative. (See CEMAM Reports, Vol. 1, No. 1 (Sept. 1973) pp. 135-8). Repercussions of this affair continued though January and February.

2) April 10, 1973 Israeli commandos landed in Beirut and assassinated early in the morning three prominent Palestinian leaders. The Prime Minister Saib Salam resigned the same day because of differences with the Army Chief of Staff about the delay in the Lebanese Army's immediate counterattack against the Israeli intrusion.

The Islamic Council of Lebanon complained of the lack of security against Israeli attacks and the lack of protection for the Palestinian Resistance. (YOM 10/4/73 p. 8). The Islamic Associations and Boards issued a statement calling for the trial of those responsible for inaction. (YOM 12/4/73 p. 10). Presumably the meeting at which this statement was drafted is the first meeting, at the headquarters of al-Hayāt al-Wataniyya, referred to in the text.

3) On April 18, Dr. Amīn al-Hafiz was appointed Prime Minister. He selected as Ministers in his Cabinet (which was formed on April 25) two young Sunnite Muslims who were not considered adequately to represent the Muslim community. Complaints were made by the Islamic Associations and Boards. (YOM 27/4/73 pp. 1 ff.; and 28/4 pp. 1, 10). However, some other Muslim political figures rejected these complaints. (N 29/4 p. 2)

4) After a rally (referred to by Amīn al-ᶜAraisi) at the headquarters of al-Hay'āt al-Wataniyya on May 4, the Executive Committee of the Islamic Organizations and Associations issued a statement which said that
(1) the authority practices a policy of individual decision (i. e., without "participation");
(2) The new Prime Minister should insist on taking part in the government not just as a figurehead; he should protect the rights of those he represents;
(3) The government should investigate the feeble resistance to the Israeli raid of April 10;
(4) We are against any Prime Minister who does not include a strong defence policy and compulsory military service in his program;
(5) we ask the new Prime Minister to fulfill Muslim demands, especially regarding the Friday holiday;
(6) Ministers and Deputies should carry out their responsibilities and be accountable; otherwise they lose the confidence of the people; and
(7) the retiring Prime Minister should reveal the reasons for his resignation. (SHIH 1/5 p. 2)

5) On May 2 fighting broke out between the Lebanese army and the Palestinian Resistance. On May 8 Dr. Hafiz signed a proclamation of a state of emergency, and, on the same day, be resigned.

6) On May 19 Dr. Hafiz withdrew his resignation, a

move which aroused opposition among those Muslims who had been critical of him.

7) The Prime Minister called for a vote of confidence by the Parliament at a session to be held in June 12. Muslim organizations reacted by a declaration calling for his resignation and for the boycotting of the vote of confidence.

That declaration, issued as a result of a meeting of delegates on 23/3 (see NAH 24/5 p. 10), also 1) said that every Muslim deputy or minister who would take part in the vote of confidence would be considered as being outside the "Islamic will"; and 2) asked Muslim personalities not to take part in the government except on the basis of the National Pact of Islamic Associations of 1955 (which assures the application of the National Pact of 1943 and of the Constitution).

8) These demands were repeated at a meeting at the headquarters of the Najjāda Party on 26/5. (OJ 27/5 pp. 1, 12; N. p. 1).

Islamic Associations also met on 30/5, confirmed the statement of 26/5, formed a committee to revise the Islamic Pact of 1955, and took a decision on seven secret paragraphs concerning the future stage of affairs. (MUH 31/5 p. 12; N. p. 1).

9) On June 12 the session of Parliament was not held. Dr. Hafiz resigned on June 14.

THREE SHIITE DOCUMENTS:

4. THE SHIITE "PACT" OF JUNE 22, 1973
5. LETTER OF IMAM MUSA SADR TO THE MEMBERS OF THE SUPREME ISLAMIC COUNCIL, DECEMBER 1973.
6. THE MEMORANDUM TO THE PRIME MINISTER TAKIEDDIN SOLH ON SHIITE DEMANDS, JULY 1973.

INTRODUCTION:

Document 4. This seems to be the first such pledge of Shiite deputies and ministers to work for the full rights of the Shiite community. It is briefer than the Sunnite pact, but at the same time more extensive in that it includes socio-economic goals. Indirectly it also indicates the political division in the community, for the deputies who did not sign the pact are : Kāmel al-As^{c}ad (President of the Chamber), Fahmi Shāhīn, Hamid Dakrūb, Anwar Sabāh, Mamdūh Abdallah and Abdul-Latif Beydūn.

Document 5. The convocation on December 10 was within the framework of the Supreme Islamic Shiite Council, which is composed of 13 ulema, 19 deputies and 12 elected members. (HAY 7/12 p. 3). The Council decided to call a general assembly within two months and to keep the Council meeting open. A second meeting on December 17 revealed a division of opinion on the action to be taken, but finished with a decision to grant the government a two month period of grace to fulfill Shiite demands. In the report on this second meeting reference is made to the accord of July 3 rather than to the June 22 pact. It appears that an emergency meeting on July 3 confirmed the pact and placed it in the framework of the Supreme Council.

Document 6. The Memorandum of Shiite demands specifies more clearly the socio-economic concerns of the community.

4. THE SHIITE "PACT" OF JUNE 22, 1973

TEXT:[+]

We, deputies of the Islamic Shiite community gathered together in the House (bayt) of the Islamic Shiite Community, pledge and obligate ourselves to work to give the Shiite community its full rights in all the institutions of the State and to eliminate backwardness from the areas (where the community is found). Our Ministers who will participate in the government pledge themselves to execute this desire of ours within a delay no longer than four months after the government receives the vote of confidence, obligating themselves to resign from the government in case these just demands are not realized. Likewise we, the undersigned deputies, also pledge ourselves not to participate, in their place, in the government and not to accept any ministerial post as long as the community has not attained its rights. Similarly we all pledge ourselves to withdraw support from every government that does not obligate itself to give the sons of the Islamic Shiite Community, their rights. This is a pledge we impose on ourselves before God, our conscience and the people.

June 22, 1973

Signed:

Sabri Hamāde (Minister), Adel Osseyrān, Kāzem Khalīl (Minister), Ali Khalīl (Minister), Abdel Latīf Zein, Mohammed Yūssef Beydūn, Mahmūd Amer, Ahmad Asbar, Hussayn Hussayni, Sobhi Yaghi, Abdel Mawla Amhaz, Hussayn Mansūr, Yūssef Hamūd.

+from al-Nahar, 11 December 1973, p. 6.

5. LETTER OF IMAM MUSA SADR TO THE MEMBERS OF THE SUPREME ISLAMIC SHIITE COUNCIL.

TEXT:+

You certainly remember that the majority of the deputies within this Council bound themselves during the meeting of 22/6/73 to strive to obtain for the community all its rights: to have an equal part in the offices of the state and to put an end to the backwardness of the regions of the community.

This was the first time in the history of the community that they (these representatives) reached a firm solidarity in the fulfillment of their obligations. It was a written and signed agreement by which they put themselves under the obligation, the ministers among them, to resign, and the deputies, in their turn, not to cooperate with the Cabinet, if this lofty aim was not realized within four months from the date on which the government obtained the confidence of the Parliament.

The present government obtained a vote of confidence on Thursday 3/8/1973. So the first day, four months from that date, is 3/12/73.

However, the rights of the Shi'ite community in the offices of the State are still what they were and the backwardness of the regions of the community is increasing every day. Here we have a symptom which indicates that this injustice in the different spheres and fields is a permanent one and is always growing. All the efforts that have been made over a long period of time to handle this situation have failed, although initiatives came from different directions and various means have been used. Some of these led us to make the greatest possible sacrifices; moreover, the efforts were made in a well-studied way to bring an end to this national distress.

For this reason I call you to attend a meeting of the two committees, the legislative and the executive, at 4 p.m. on Monday 10/12/73, 15 dhu al-qa^{c}dah 1393, at the assembly room of the Supreme Islamic Shi'ite Council, to examine the agenda included in this letter, being assured of the importance you will give to this meeting.

+from al-Hayat, 7 December, 1973, p. 3.

6. MEMORANDUM PRESENTED TO PRIME MINISTER TAKIEDDIN AL-SOLH BY SHAIKH ABDAL-AMIR QABALAN, JAFARITE (SHIITE) MUFTI AND MEMBER OF THE SUPREME ISLAMIC SHIITE COUNCIL, EXPOSING THE DEMANDS OF THE SHIITE COMMUNITY.

TEXT:+

In as much as you have been in the vanguard of those who feel deeply the deprivation which affects the South and in particular the Islamic Shiite Community (tā'ifa), and in as much as you were the first to turn your concern to this area and this community, we have come now to help focus your attention, by way of a reminder, on some of the demands which are pressing at the present time. We can summarize them as follows:

- just treatment of the Islamic Shiite community by giving it its full rights in the area of general government employment;

- reinstatement of the teachers dismissed from their posts;

- indemnity for those killed, wounded and harmed by the course of recent events;

- provision of the necessary credits for the Council for the South so that it can continue to execute the projects which it has drawn up;

- serious concern for the irrigation project for the South and the other development projects which are aimed at the development, prosperity and progress of this area;

- serious concern for the developmental, social, cultural and economic projects for the area of Baalbek, Hermel, and the other areas which still suffer from backwardness and deprivation.

+from al-Hayat, 29 July 1973, p. 2.

Printed at the
IMPRIMERIE CATHOLIQUE, BEIRUT
September 1974

Since 1964 DAR EL-MASHREQ has been the title of the publishing house of the Catholic Press (l'Imprimerie Catholique) in Beirut. Founded in 1852, the Press has excelled in the quality of its craftsmanship and in the variety of material that has issued from its presses. Perhaps the most celebrated and influential publication of the Press has been Louis Cheikho's Arabic periodical, *el-Mashreq* (1898-1970). Some of the works published or printed at the Press are:

Munjed Dictionaries

Standard references for many years, these dictionaries are now being completely revised. Two have just been published, the Arabic-Arabic and the French-Arabic, while the third, the English-Arabic, will appear shortly.

Publications of Saint Joseph's University, Beirut (P.O.B. 293)

* *Mélanges de l'Université Saint-Joseph* (formerly *Mélanges de la Faculté Orientale de Beyrouth,* founded in 1906) edited by Maurice Tallon, 46 volumes by Oriental specialists on Semitic and other languages (Arabic, Hebrew, Syriac, Coptic, and Ethiopic), on religious and secular history, and on the geography, archeology and epigraphy of the Near East.
* *Recherches,* founded in 1956, published by the Institute of Oriental Letters, and edited by Paul Nwyia. A collection of outstanding Oriental studies produced by members of the Institute and its collaborators. Over 50 volumes include works written or edited by such authorities as Selim Abou, Michel Allard, Antoine Fattal, Henri Fleisch, Camille Hechaîme, George Makdisi, Muhsin Mahdi and Paul Nwyia.
* *Proche-Orient, Études juridiques* (15 volumes) and
* *Proche-Orient, Études économiques* (12 volumes), Jean Ducruet, editor; concerned, respectively, with Middle East law and economics (formerly *Annales de la Faculté de Droit et des Sciences économiques,* 1945-1967, 49 volumes). Also,
* *Documents Huvelin,* a bilingual (Arabic-French) series on Lebanese law, with volumes on *Statut Personnel* and *Code de Commerce.* These series on law and economics are published by the Faculty of Law and Economics, P.O.B. 293, Beirut.

Publications of the University Cultural Center
(Centre Culturel Universitaire, P.O.B. 946, Beirut)

* *Travaux et Jours* (René Chamussy, editor), a quarterly periodical devoted to issues of current social concern.
* *Hommes et Société du Proche-Orient* (Selim Abou, editor), a collection of studies, in print or in press, by Emile J.P. Valin, Richard Alouche, Roland Meynet, Mounir Chamoun, Jean Brun and Olivier Carré.

Printing for Other Universities and Institutions

The Press produces high quality printing for many other universities and scholarly institutions, such as: American University of Beirut, The Institute for Palestine Studies, Institut Français d'Études Arabes de Damas, The Lebanese University, New York State University, Orient-Institut der Deutschen Morgenländischen Gesellschaft, Otto Harrassowitz Verlag, Université de Provence, and University of Libya.

DAR EL-MASHREQ PUBLISHERS
P.O.B. 946, Beirut, Lebanon

Distributor:
LIBRAIRIE ORIENTALE
P.O.B. 1986, Beirut, Lebanon